OUT OF STEAM

K4

Please return or renew this item before the latest date shown below

Renewals can be made
by internet   www.onfife.com/fife-libraries
in person   at any library in Fife
by phone   03451 55 00 66

ON
AT FIFE
LIBRARIES

Thank you for using your library

OUT OF STEAM

The Beeching years in hindsight

Robert Adley

PSL

PATRICK STEPHENS LIMITED

First published in 1990

British Library Cataloguing in Publication Data
Adley, Robert
Out of steam: the Beeching years in hindsight.
1. Great Britain. Railway services: British Rail, history
I. Title
385'.0941

ISBN 1-85260-202-3

Front endpaper
Birkenhead Woodside on 22 May 1965 (see page 30).
Title page
Between Godstone and Edenbridge, the SECR Redhill-Tonbridge line crosses two arms of the LB & SCR: Oxted-East Grinstead and Oxted-Groombridge. All these lines survive.

There was always a particular aura about such crossing-points, exemplified here as an unidentified Maunsell 'Mogul' heads the 12.11 Redhill to Tonbridge train over the LB & SCR line to East Grinstead on 23 March 1963. Surely the stream of smoke is like the wind in the flaxen hair of a nymph...

Much of the railway system in the Kent-Surrey-Sussex border country has been decimated; that which somehow survived is being modernized and electrified. The moral is clear.
Rear endpaper
The interregnum between steam and diesel at Paddington, January 1963 (see page 73).

Patrick Stephens Limited is part of the Thorsons Publishing Group, Wellingborough, Northamptonshire NN8 2RQ, England.

Printed in Great Britain by William Collins Sons & Co. Ltd, Glasgow
Typesetting by MJL Limited, Hitchin, Hertfordshire.

10 9 8 7 6 5 4 3 2 1

ACKNOWLEDGEMENTS

To Simon and Rupert for their research; Jane for her tolerance; Kay Dixon for her ingenuity in deciphering my hieroglyphics; and Peter Semmens for correcting and adjusting the manuscript.

To the French Embassy in London, to the French Department of Transport and to SNCF; and to all those who have allowed me openly to quote their views — my sincere thanks.

CONTENTS

INTRODUCTION

Hero or villain, butcher or surgeon, far-sighted reformer or dog-matic destroyer: such are the contradictory descriptions heaped on the head of the late Lord Beeching. The name of the scientist-cum-civil-servant-cum-businessman, translated by Transport Minister Ernest Marples from Technical Director of ICI into the Chairmanship of the British Transport Commission, has now become an established word in the English dictionary, albeit frequently adjectivally attached to words like 'axe'. Therein lies the rub: for when he assumed overall control of Britain's railways on 1 June 1961, the end was nigh for the benevolent post-nationalization style of management which had existed since the demise of the 'Big Four' railways following the state's take-over and the formation of British Railways.

Dr Beeching's name is forever linked in the minds of Britain's railway enthusiasts with the demise of the beloved steam engine and with the closure of thousands of miles of railway line; indeed, the British branch line as we knew and loved it is often assumed to have been truncated single-handedly by 'the Doctor'. Is this a fair legacy for the man?

Steam motive power, and branchline idyll, are the two most mourned features of the railway scene for lovers of the railway. The demise of the former, and the decimation of the latter, are the visible and lasting manifestations of the 'Beeching era'. Examinations of the impact of Beeching on the railway scene, a quarter of a century later, are either curiously dismissive of the man's role, or are encompassed within detailed and voluminous studies of the commercial history of British Railways. In the former category, often produced by enthusiasts without regard to the context within which he undertook his task, he is given little credit for the essential reshaping of railway management, or of the equally essential redefinition both of the role of the railway and/or its relationship with the Government of the day. In the latter category, his role is usually examined within the framework of detailed, minuted, thoroughly researched publications from which the spirit of the railway, its soul, has been cauterized. For some of these authors, financial factors and balance sheets are as irrelevant in assessing Beeching as are the social factors and the humanitarian needs and considerations

Opposite On 14 November 1965, Stanier 2-6-4T No 42606 pounds up the grade from Birkenhead Woodside towards Rock Ferry with the 14.55 Birkenhead to Paddington train. The first through train ran on this route on 10 October 1861, the last on 5 March 1967.

Woodside has now been obliterated through re-development. The demise of genuinely competitive routes from Merseyside to London, either from Liverpool to Euston or by the GWR & LNWR Joint route seen here, is one factor to which those who demand the privatization of BR are oblivious; and one reason why some of their comments about 'competition' are so asinine to those who know what has happened to much of our railway system.

For me, this photograph epitomizes the appeal of the steam railway. I can still hear the crisp two-cylinder beat matching the exhaust as the engine, with express passenger headlamps, pounds towards me. The paraphernalia of the railway is all around, and one of Liverpool's cathedrals is visible on the right background.

to their contemporary scribes. Between the two, and with the benefit not only of hindsight but also the twin hats of enthusiast and parliamentarian, steps the present author. He is much aided by Richard Hardy's book, *Beeching: Champion of the Railway?*, which emanates from the pen of a Beeching fan. Yet, as just one example, he tell us that 'Whilst on the Stedeford Committee and subsequently, Beeching had opposed the extension of electrification to Glasgow. Changing engines was a laborious business, the replacement diesels were by no means reliable in the early 1970s and when electrification eventually came in 1973, railwaymen (and others) breathed a sigh of relief.'

Attitudes towards railways are at present in the midst of a significant change. Congestion, pollution and environmental factors win the railway ever more friends, whilst modern, professional yet committed management can capitalize on a generally supportive public. Yet, tucked away in the recesses of Whitehall and Westminster are the enemies of the railway. They can be identified in shorthand as the 'Roads Lobby' and the 'Anti-Nationalization Fanatics'. The former, whose tactics we shall look at shortly, are motivated by money, either as operators of road transport or as that industry's lobbyists. The latter, mainly but not exclusively on the far right of British politics, believe quite simply that 'if it's nationalized, it's useless'.

It is impossible to write about the impact of the Beeching era without being political. I hope, however — indeed I am sure — that it will be my 'railway' rather than my 'party political' prejudices that permeate this book. It is important to try to prevent one's prejudices totally capturing one's pen. Charity towards one's opponents is not always an overt characteristic of the politician, and it is an old adage that, in the House of Commons, one's opponents sit opposite, one's 'enemies' sit beside and behind! Thus, but without malice, it is relevant to record the words of T.R. Gourvish in his *British Railways 1949-73*: 'Beeching was appointed to give effect to government intentions for its largest loss-maker by a Minister bent on redirecting resources into road transport'.

How does the 'Rail Lobby' compete with the 'Road Lobby'? Is it a secret ambition of some politicians to close down, or to privatize, the railways? This is an essentially 'political' question, of only passing interest to enthusiasts, and 'railway politics' as a subject is unlikely to captivate and enthral the traditional purchasers of railway books. Books that are written by authors who can say 'The crux of BR's initial problem was that the assets it took over were, in terms of their aggregate earning power, worthless' and, with reference to nationalization, 'We can see now, of course, that the railway assets were worthless in terms of their earning power', seem unlikely to become 'Editor's Choice' of the Railway Book Club. That such statements as these, by Dr Stewart Joy in *The Train that Ran Away*, can be justified in a dry, unemotional, financial assessment of the railway in society is not in dispute. It is no part of my intention to criticize the views of other authors; but it *is* my intention to make clear that this is not that style of book.

Critical I can certainly be, of railway management and of ministerial intentions; but I am committed to 'the railway' to a degree that probably prevents me from fulfilling the role of dispassionate author. Indeed, I make no apology for a passionate attachment to the railway, and that is why it is the 'railway-operational' facets of Beeching that will feature principally herein — the motive power and route-operating aspects of the post-Beeching era, as seen through the eyes and lens of a dedicated enthusiast. It is a book aimed at fellow enthusiasts and not at fellow politicians; a book from which there is little serious attempt totally to exclude my prejudices and partial affections. Indeed, my re-entry into the world of active enthusiasm, in the years 1962-68, ensured — and this is seen only now, with hindsight, as I set out to write this book — that this re-entry coincided with the era of visible implementation of the Beeching policies. Thus where my previous books have tended to align anecdote with my photographs, it is the attempt to set them in their historical perspective, in railway operating and in political terms, that this one strives to achieve.

Hero or villain, butcher or surgeon? Perhaps if we are to encapsulate, to capture, the spirit of Beeching dispassionately, we could claim for him the proposition that '50 per cent of something is better than 100 per cent of nothing'. That today's railway is healthy, that capital investment is much in evidence, that the Chairman of the Board — at the time of writing — is a railwayman, much respected not only by the Transport Minister but by the Prime Minister herself, is itself a legacy of Beeching's reform of the structure of BR. This is not an eulogy, merely a thought — a thought born of an attempt to link the railway scene of today with the Beeching years that ended in May 1965, although, of course, the effects of Beeching lasted years beyond his departure.

In that month, with but three years to go before the end of steam, my interest was largely confined to the motive power itself, although I did occasionally photograph, for its own sake, the melancholy view of lines from which services had been withdrawn, the track lifted, the weeds flexing their muscles. Awareness of impending doom was not frequently a major factor in determining my choice of photographic locations, although a year earlier just such an impetus drew me to Woodford Halse.

The decision to close the most modern of all the main lines to London, the erstwhile Great Central, was perhaps inevitable. Shunted from one region to another, and in direct competition with the Midland and the North Western lines, it never really had a chance of surviving the 'Beeching Rules'. Had it remained *in situ*, what would have been the fate of the Great Central today? Would not Woodford Halse, rail-connected, have been an excellent candidate for a new town? And what about the destruction of those invaluable — or now seen as invaluable by some — routes and lines in areas of major growth where the motor car, lorry and coach are inexorably choking civilization? Beeching's

Overleaf *Two months after photographing DP2 at Camden my camera caught an example of an unsung hero from pre-First World War days, on shed at Southall. Churchward 2-6-0 No 6350 was a member of the Great Western '43xx' Class introduced in 1911. With a tender full of 'nuts', the juxtapositioning of photographs illustrates better than words the interregnum inherent in the transition from steam to diesel. It is 30 June 1963, and No 6350 — built in 1923 and withdrawn in 1964 — epitomizes the filthy, uncared-for state of the declining steam stock. Locomotives were allowed, literally, to grind to a halt before being withdrawn; little wonder that recollections of steam's final years are tinged with sadness that reliable machinery was condemned to such an ignominious end.*

Woodford Halse epitomizes the Great Central, and the Great Central epitomizes unforgivable vandalism of our railway heritage. '8F' 2-8-0 No 48336 of Woodford (1G) stands in front of her crumbling home shed in the pouring rain on 6 June 1964.

appointment, two years after the 'You've-never-had-it-so-good' election, coincided with the explosion of popular motoring. Who could have then foreseen, as many indeed have not even yet foreseen, that the form of 'motive power' that was responsible for the assault on and the near demise of the passenger railway, namely the internal combustion engine, may yet become the *raison d'être* of its renaissance?

Whilst in Britain trains have changed, and track has disappeared, what has been happening across the Channel? From the Haut Pyrénées to Brittany, rural lines serving remote villages, and branches stretching from obscure junctions to isolated communities, have survived: survived not on Beechingesque, but on Gallic commitment. If there is something ambivalent about a nation that simultaneously develops cheap nuclear energy whilst maintaining a vast cobweb of economically unjustifiable railway lines, then long live ambivalence.

The French remain *committed* to their railway system in a manner that has never, since the golden years of the railway, been emulated here. Whilst they developed the TGV, investing hundreds of millions of pounds in a chain of 'rail-motorways', we fiddled and fumbled with the Advanced Passenger Train, finally starving it to death. We have produced the High Speed Train, but certainly no new high-speed rail-way. On one side of the Channel Tunnel, SNCF prepares to capitalize on a new era of rail potential, whilst in Britain we make Dr Beeching seem like a reckless adventurer as the Government squeezes BR's ability to do likewise. The Redhill-Reading line, taken over from the Reading, Guildford & Reigate Company by the South Eastern Railway in 1852 with the Channel Tunnel in mind, was retained by Beeching in spite of its failure to meet his criteria for retention. This was due to his estimation that it would eventually be a vital part of the Channel Tunnel link, yet it is not, as I write, due to be electrified and fully utilized within the BR scheme for Tunnel traffic, due to its inability to meet the grotesque criteria forced on BR by the Government.

All is not gloom, however. Out of the leaner but unquestionably fitter railway have come schemes dreamed of for generations but now a reality, like the electrification of the East Coast Main Line and the construction of the Windsor Link in Manchester. All round the country, people are awakening to the fact that rail transport is the best and, in most cases, the only answer to urban congestion. Let me take an example from my own experience as Member of Parliament for Bristol North-East, elected in 1970. The ritual antagonism 'twixt the Midland Railway and the Great Western between Bristol and Birmingham resulted ultimately in the Western Region gaining control of this trunk route. With little love lost, and in complying with Government policy to sacrifice lines whenever possible, the erstwhile Midland line from Bristol, through Fishponds and Mangotsfield, was closed. At the latter place the line made a triangular junction with the line through Warmley to Bath, whilst the line to Gloucester turned north to Yate. The population of this area has mushroomed since then; the railway has gone for ever. However, at the time I put forward a scheme for developing existing under-utilized lines, plus lines closed, plus lines extant but with track lifted, as well as lines in use only for freight, in a planned urban rail infrastructure.

The *Bristol Evening Post* of 21 July 1971, under the heading 'Save the Severn Beach Rail Line — Adley', recalls in print my first successful attempt to generate press interest in my concept of creating an integrated rail network serving what is now the County of Avon. The basis of my scheme was simple: keep the existing lines open; reopen to passenger traffic those lines now used only for freight; reinstate lines where track has been lifted, but the track-bed is *in situ*; and, in one or two places, construct spurs or short sections of new line. The article continued, ' "Bristol is road-mad," Mr Adley declared. "I fear that if we close this line down we will find ourselves in ten years time rubbing our hands with remorse and asking ourselves how we did not have the sense to keep it open." Mr Adley said a distinction should be drawn between straggling country train services and urban branch lines carrying mainly commuter and shopping traffic. Severn Beach had considerable potential. "If the railways would do a little more to attract new traffic from

Overleaf Built over a century ago with the Channel Tunnel in mind, yet today unable to meet Government criteria for electrification, the Reading-Redhill line was spared by Beeching yet spurned by Thatcher. GWR 'Manor' 4-6-0 No 7816 Frilsham Manor characterizes the inter-regional role of the line as, with Southern stock, she mounts the 1 in 99 bank and heads for Dorking with train number IV86 on 20 July 1963.

Above *On the erstwhile Midland line 'twixt Bristol, Gloucester and Birmingham, Fishponds Station, seen in August 1969, illustrates the solid and spacious nature of the stations in the Bristol area. Modern traction would indubitably have regenerated rail transport in such areas, but short-sighted politicians deemed otherwise.*

Opposite *The S & D line from Highbridge to Bason Bridge, across the Somerset levels, was the last piece of this marvellous route to remain in use, operating in fact as a branch from the GWR line at Highbridge to the milk factory. The service survived for some time after 'The Branch' — and indeed the main S & D line — succumbed finally on 7 March 1966. On 18 August 1963, GWR '2251' Class 0-6-0 No 2204 has charge of the milk tanks at Bason Bridge. Now, of course, the railway has gone, the milk traffic was transferred from rail to road, and finally the factory, too, has closed.*

areas which had been opened up to the line through recent road development, they would find that the potential for the line was considerable." '

My effort to prevent closure was successful. Few in Bristol today remember that the line was once scheduled to close. Sadly, I was less successful in my well-reported attempts to save the former Midland Railway line from Bristol to Bath via Mangotsfield and to Yate. Mindful of current — and continuing — exhortations by Government to BR to sell off land in order to raise revenue, one cannot but recall that little changes: an article in the *Evening Post* of 20 April 1972, written around a letter to me from the Department of the Environment, opens with the sentence: 'Plans to reopen the rail route linking Bristol, Bath and Yate new town are in danger of being wrecked because of moves by British Railways to sell the land, it was disclosed this afternoon.' One of the local politicians, subsequently knighted, told me 'there is no road traffic problem in Bristol'. Now, others have 'lifted' my ideas, dusted them down and made some progress; still the local authorities lack enthusiasm, although it may be that the personalities involved, rather than the proposals, are the cause of the problem.

So, the twin tracks of mistaken policy revolve around inadequate contemplation of future patterns of growth of population and its movement, together with a short-term policy of selling off land and thus precluding use of said land in the light of changed patterns of growth and travel. In fact, the growth and development of the motorway system has, ironically, created new opportunity for development of the railway system. For example, the M4 has seen major growth at Reading and Swindon; the M1 at Milton Keynes (with a new station, but certainly no new rail links) and Northampton; the M5 at Redditch. But there has been no new rail construction to link these places. Indeed, many of the cross-country rail links that were destroyed would have been invaluable today. Of course, hindsight is the easiest form of vision, but why, oh why, were we — indeed, are we — so myopic about our railways?

No book of mine can be complete without reference to the Somerset & Dorset Joint Railway. At the southern end, Blandford (see page 77) and Wimborne badly need, but will never again have, the railway that once served these very busy and prosperous towns. With local government reorganization dramatically affecting social, commercial and even political movement following the 1972 Local Government Act, transportation from south and east Dorset through the county and through Somerset has grown unimaginably since the closure of the S & D in 1966. Even places like Bason Bridge, on 'the Branch' to Highbridge and Burnham-on-Sea, now dominated by the M5 Motorway and its traffic, could surely have used this erstwhile rail connection.

What of the future? Can we not anticipate growth areas? Can we not detect travel patterns? We are constantly told that more houses are needed in the South-East. We can see vast tracks of derelict land in East London, around Beckton. We know that it is Government policy to regenerate areas of urban decay whilst seeking to protect the Green Belt. Simultaneously we are building the Channel Tunnel. It is Government policy to seek to bring the greatest advantage of the Tunnel to regions distant from it. To do this, we must provide improved rail links to Scotland and Northern England. Good travel facilities — not just roads — are an essential ingredient in ensuring the success of new urban development.

Overleaf *The water-tower and shed at Highbridge host GWR '57xx' 0-6-0PT No 4631 and LMS 'Ivatt' 2-6-2T No 41208 on 20 February 1965. The demise of the Somerset & Dorset Joint Railway caused more grief than any BR closure. There is but a year to go here before the process of elimination of virtually all trace of the railway will begin.*

1
WHO NEEDS A RAILWAY?

'In the new world of science and finance, and particularly of democratic and semi-socialised forms of government in which we now live, transport occupies a more important place than ever, and the position of railways in the economic structure of all countries requires to be re-examined without prejudices from the past, but losing none of its lessons.'

Railways, W. V. Wood and Sir Josiah Stamp, 1928

Some people 'believe' in railways, much as others believe in homeopathic medicine. Those of us who are disciples of the iron way are convinced that the railway offers the only solution to the problems of overcrowding, congestion and pollution which are inherent in the towns and cities and on the motorways of this small island. Few of us — members of the Brotherhood of Rail, formerly the Brotherhood of Steam — are so blinkered as to deny the proper role of roads and the internal combustion engine. We fear, however, the possibility, indeed the probability, that unfettered growth of road traffic cannot be permitted, save at the expense of civilized living.

For 150 years, the railway has provided a separated style of travel that does not fill pedestrians' noses with fumes; that does not undermine the fabric of our ancient buildings; that does not kill 5,000 or maim 250,000 people each and every year; and does not gobble up acres of land inexorably. Attitudes to the railway are changing and more and more people imagine that another 'Railway Age' — and indeed a related 'Tramway Age' — is approaching. If these hopes are to be fulfilled, we must succeed in challenging the long-accepted 'advantages' assumed to lie with road transport. Legislation and regulation, long prognosticated in favour of roads, must be reviewed. Britain needs the railways it has, more than ever. Indeed, Britain needs more railways; we need a new Railway Age.

Personal priorities in transport can only be resolved by exercising choice. How far, however, can or should people's personal predilections be financed by the taxpayer? Why should some forms of public transport be provided on roads funded out of general taxation, whilst alternative forms of public transport are provided by a body that is expected to provide its own 'roads'? By what logic or fairness can a private-sector coach operator, plying, shall we say, between London and Birmingham, have all but his direct operating costs borne by the taxpayer, whilst the competing railway has to bear all its direct operating costs?

With today's rise in personal mobility determined by economic growth, and with environmental concerns simultaneously increasing, there has to be some form of planning and co-ordination of land transport in this country. Dogmatic political arguments about ownership are sterile and irrelevant. Even Rupert Murdoch's *The Times* newspaper, an enthusiastic supporter of market forces and what is known as the 'enterprise culture', now recognizes that transport cannot be left to resolve its own problems without recognition of its wholly exceptional role in the national life. In a leading article on 4 November 1988, commenting on the report of the National Audit Office (NAO) about the gross inaccuracies of the Department of Transport's forecasting of road traffic flows, the question was raised that railway enthusiasts have sought in vain to raise for so many years, namely the need to re-examine the cost-benefit criteria of investment in road as opposed to rail:

'How far, for example, do the cost-benefit equations used by the

Long before the wires came to modernize the East Coast Main Line, stations like Hitchin had goods yards and local freight traffic aplenty. However, from my memory of this day in February 1964, LNER 'B1' 4-6-0 No 61109 was performing the last rites in the vicinity of Hitchin Shed, which had closed in June 1961. Few if any colour shots at this location have been published — although 'colour' is not much in evidence, the locomotive's appearance speaking for itself. The shed did duty for 111 years, being opened by the Great Northern Railway in 1850. No 61109 was withdrawn a few weeks later and was cut up at King's, Norwich, in October 1964.

Department of Transport reflect comparisons between modes of transport? How far do they relate the public investment in rail to that in road? Why do they exclude unit cost estimates — the benefit conferred on individual users of the highways? The latter calculation will have to be made if any kind of toll scheme is ever to be approved.

'The NAO also misses what must now be a central issue in road planning: to what extent the demand from motorists, cars and lorries ought to be treated as something which is subject to its own rules and cannot be influenced. The existence of the London orbital motorway — we now know well — creates extra traffic.

'Transport *planning* may involve thinking the hitherto unthinkable: schemes to ration available road space in an effort to constrain and maybe even cut the use of vehicles; maybe *not* building roads where greater congestion would be generated. The gravest charge that can be laid at the door of the Department of Transport is that it seems to have given up thinking such heretical thoughts.'

So what chance is there of a full and honest cost-benefit analysis as between road and rail? How does one assess the 'cost' of death, for example? What factors should be included in this assessment?

Reference to Chapter 5 compares the regime existing in France to that pertaining here. Roads gobble up infinitely more land; cost much more to build; generate immeasurably more pollution and congestion; kill and maim countless tens of thousands; create untold costs for the National Health Service; involve millions of hours of time for police and courts annually; and have virtually everything funded by the taxpayer. Traffic wardens, whose job was created by, with and from the 'road industry', have 7 per cent of their time allocated to 'road costs', the remaining 93 per cent to general taxation. The railway, in terms of cost/benefit to the nation, scores endlessly on such comparisons — yet even has to pay for its own police force. Yet, in spite of this, a graph of the last 30 years, as shown opposite, indicating what has actually happened, makes food for thought.

What is the reason for this inequality of liability assessment? Indeed, is there any such 'inequality'? What is the difference, in real terms, between a privately-owned operator and a state-owned operator? The distribution of operating costs is still assessed between the perceived 'users' or 'beneficiaries' and the provider of the funding, namely the 'shareholder' either as individual or as taxpayer. These are fundamental questions, inextricably bound up with politics in its broadest sense. As ever, there are extremes of view — or there would be to those who have studied the question, as presumably someone has. These extremes might be set out in the political context of 'left' and 'right' as outlined overleaf.

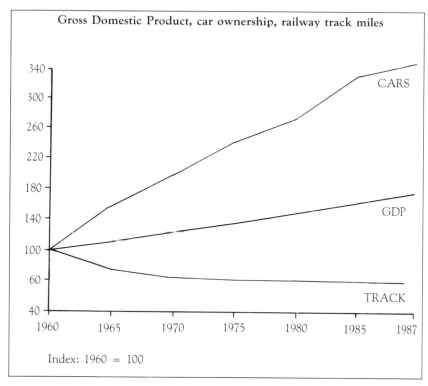

Gross Domestic Product, car ownership, railway track miles

Index: 1960 = 100

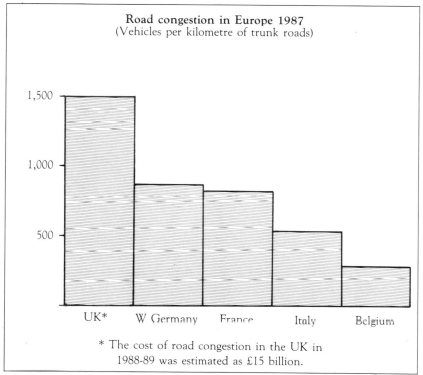

Road congestion in Europe 1987
(Vehicles per kilometre of trunk roads)

* The cost of road congestion in the UK in
1988-89 was estimated as £15 billion.

Left: Transport should be provided free at the point of movement, funded out of general taxation where each has paid according to his means.

Right: Transport should be provided at the point of movement to those who can afford to pay for it, and the price they pay shall be borne entirely by those who use the service.

Neither of these propositions is acceptable to me. The first, or 'left', would pay no regard to the efficient use of limited resources. The second, or 'right', would take no account of assessment of needs, or of the public interest.

As one's mind ponders the extent of Government control over the railways, the obligations laid upon them, and the assumptions about their being an essential part of the fabric of our society, one cannot escape the conclusion that comparisons 'twixt public transport by rail alongside the competitors by road and air — *public* transport, not private, owner-driven — are totally inappropriate and unfair unless an 'x' factor is included as compensation for the railway's public obligations. How extensive are these obligations and how far do they extend beyond the legislative requirement that seeks to ensure safety for the passenger?

As early in the railway era as 1842, Parliament passed The Better Regulation of Railways and for the Conveyance of Troops Act. Under this legislation, the railway companies were compelled to provide conveyance for troops and military necessities at specified maximum fares and rates. In 1867 these provisions were extended to the Army Reserve, and in 1883 they were further amended by the Cheap Trains Act.

It was not long before the *de facto* indispensability of the railway system was recognized by the Government taking unto itself powers of actual control in time of war. In 1871, under provisions of the Regulation of the Forces Act, and again in 1888, in the National Defence Act, legislation was passed to achieve this objective. The powers were draconian and far from clear. However, it *is* clear that after the 1871 Act was passed, the Secretary for War, Edward Cardwell, is purported to have stated that the powers entrusted to him under the Act were excessive and unneccessary, and would never be used.

However, 20 years in the House of Commons has taught me not to expect Governments lightly to relinquish powers they have acquired. When the 1888 Act appeared there was no repeal of Section 16 of the 1871 legislation. Indeed, Section 4 of the National Defence Act was, by Order in Council in 1908, extended to the Territorials. That confusion existed as between the provisions of the Acts of 1871 and 1888 is not in dispute by students of railway history. The risk of such confusion, should the powers need to be exercised, was far from theoretical; they concerned the extent and manner under which Ministerial control might be exercised, ranging literally from take-over, dismissal of existing staff and their replacement by Government appointees to merely — I use the word in comparative terms — the right to exercise claims for priority of traffic.

With storm clouds appearing, albeit distantly on the horizon, at the beginning of the second decade of this century, the major railway companies — LNWR, GWR, MR, GNR, GCR, and LSWR — sought clarification of their position. They suggested the formation of a permanent body representing the railway companies on the one hand and the various Government departments involved — War Office, Admiralty, Home Office, Board of Trade — on the other. Thus, upon eventual acceptance by the Government of a scheme based upon these proposals, there emerged the first faltering steps towards Government control of Britain's railways. If, however, a man like Sir Frank Ree, erstwhile General Manager of the LNWR, or Sir Herbert Walker, latterly Chairman of the SR, were to be accused of having paved the way to nationalization, it is doubtful if their response would have been considered suitable to be heard in mixed company! Nevertheless, they became, the former in 1912 and the latter as his immediate successor, Acting Chairmen of the Railway Executive Committee. The wisdom of the General Managers in pressing for the creation of this Committee was vindicated on 4 August 1914, when an Order provided for in Section 16 of the Regulation of the Forces Act was duly made. The Prime Minister,

Opposite *The obligations laid on the railways by Parliament are reflected in the conditions laid down by BR on those seeking to operate 'private' trains on BR tracks, especially when hauled by steam. The legacy of Beeching on the erstwhile main line of the Southern Railway to Exeter and onwards is a miserable single-track route westwards from Salisbury, operated like an extended branch line.*

Amongst an army of enthusiasts who sought for years to see a steam locomotive bursting out of Buckhorn Weston tunnel, climbing the banks out of Gillingham, or sweeping round the bend at Milborne Port, we finally achieved our goal in 1986. Clan Line returned, sweet and silent, to perform every bit as well and more quietly than the wretched diesels that provide such an undistinguished service on the line. Perversity prompts me, however to select this shot of GWR 'Modified Hall' No 6998 Burton Agnes Hall, leaving, in fading light, an unforgettable trademark as she erupts from the eastern portal of Buckhorn Weston tunnel on the day's last run, the 17.27 Yeovil Junction to Salisbury train on 5 October 1986.

Birkenhead Woodside, terminus in the town centre, adjacent to the Mersey ferries, is the archetypal casualty of railway 'rationalization'. Now instead of through trains to London, travellers who formerly used the GWR/LNWR joint line from here to Paddington, via Chester, Birmingham, and Banbury, must either start their journey by crossing the Mersey to Liverpool, or struggle improbably from Birkenhead to Hooton and change: Hooton to Chester and change: Chester to Euston: and even the last link has few through trains today. Here, LMS Fairburn 2-6-4T No 42247 prepares to leave on the first leg of the soon-to-disappear Birkenhead-Paddington service, on 22 May 1965. Anyone for the steam railway?

Herbert Asquith, in his capacity also as Secretary of State for War, issued a warrant empowering the President of the Board of Trade to take possession of the railways of Britain.

The misunderstanding as between 'Government control' and 'Government administration' seems in retrospect to have differed only in concept and ambition as between 1914 and the immediate aftermath of nationalization in 1948, when the railwaymen of the GWR, LMS, LNER, and SR expected shunting on 1.1.48 to be different from shunting on 31.12.47. That, however, is another story. The point to address is this: if it can be shown that the railway, unlike other forms of transport, has a national role incomparable with its so-called 'competitors', then the most fundamental questions need to be asked. If it can be shown that, in times of national emergency, the nation needs not only railways in general, but also railways in particular, then the whole economic case for line closures may need to be re-examined. Routes like the M & SWJ, the S & D and the Great Central, to name but three, were closed as a result of Beeching on purely contemporary economic grounds. Their vital wartime role was totally ignored as a factor that could ever rise again. Will trains to the ports for military reasons ever be needed again? I wonder. Nuclear disarmament? Conventional warfare predominant? Channel Tunnel transport routes? (The Ministry of Defence is, even now, assessing the *transport* implications of the opening of the Channel Tunnel for the movement of men and materials in a conventional war scenario.) Fanciful theories, or prudent future planning? The Regulation of the Forces Act can only apply to lines that still exist...

In discussing lines taken over by the Railway Executive Committee, the following paragraph is extracted from Chapter IX of *British Railways and the Great War* by Edwin A. Pratt (Selwyn & Blount, 1921):

'A good example of these conditions is afforded by the Banbury branch of the Great Central — a nine-mile link which, opened in 1902, connects the Great Central at Woodford and Hinton with the Great Western at Banbury. Thanks to this short branch, trains from Southampton passing on to the Great Western from the London and South Western, at Basingstoke, can join the Great Central at Banbury and continue on that company's system, via Leicester, Nottingham and Sheffield, to Mexboro'. Thence they can proceed over the Swinton and Knottingly Joint line (Midland and North Eastern) to Ferrybridge, where a connection with the North Eastern allows of an extension of this through service

The last steam-operated main line in Britain was the erstwhile LSWR from Waterloo to Weymouth via Basingstoke and Southampton. On 25 September 1963 the line saw frequent and regular clean locomotives, the passenger trains mainly worked by Bulleid 'Pacifics'. On 25 September 1963, rebuilt 'West Country' No 34012 Launceston *had charge of the 14.54 Waterloo-Basingstoke train, seen here on the slow line east of Winchfield. The telegraph wires have gone, too...*

to York, Darlington, Newcastle and Scotland. Save for a slight bend towards east between Banbury and Woodford, the rail communication is in almost a straight line from Southampton to Newcastle-on-Tyne.'

A look at the railway map of 1914 alongside the system today shows that it is fervently to be hoped that there is no strategic need for this direct route. Incidentally, Knottingley itself was not actually on the S & K. This tale can be repeated on numerous other routes. Who needs a railway indeed?

In the interwar years, a campaign was waged by the 'Big Four' railway companies against the grossly unfair trading shackles imposed upon them which were not imposed upon their main competitor, the road haulage industry. On the front cover of a gem of a booklet entitled 'Fair play for the Railways' are quoted the words of the Chancellor of the Exchequer, Winston Churchill, in the House of Commons on 24 April 1928. The Chancellor stated: 'It is the duty of the State to hold the balance even between road and rail'.

Another similar campaigning booklet, published by the Railway Companies Association and entitled 'Clear the Lines', sets out very clearly the historic cause and nature of the problem of distorted and unfair competition faced, especially on the freight side, by Britain's railways. Whilst some factors have changed — for example, the discovery of North Sea oil has, with the elimination of steam haulage, rendered obsolete one of the arguments, albeit a minor one, in 'Fair Play for the Railways' — many of the circumstances remain just as relevant today. In the meantime, the Second World War crippled the railways physically and financially, and undoubtedly their reduced circumstances affected attitudes to their assumed capabilities.

During the war, the slogan, 'Is your journey really necessary?' became a popular catchphrase. It implied that travelling was an expense on the public purse, and sought to discourage the use of scarce resources. Many of today's critics of BR's post-war performance grew up in that era when the railways were suffering simultaneously from wartime exhaustion, post-war financial restrictions on investment, and the political upheaval of nationalization. Since then, the railways have never, mentally, been given a fair chance by their politically-motivated detractors.

The Labour Party's document 'Let us Face the Future', produced for the 1945 General Election, advocated the public ownership of inland transport services by rail, road, air and canal. They were described, in company with coal, gas, electricity, iron and steel, as basic industries 'ripe and over-ripe for public ownership and management in the direct service of the nation'.

For the Conservative Party, Mr Churchill's 'Declaration of Policy to the Electors' had stated: 'We should examine the conditions and the vital needs of every industry on its own merits. We believe in variety, not in standardized and identical structure, still less in bureaucratic

CLEAR THE LINE!

ALL RIGHT IN GRANDFATHER'S DAY
Ancient regulations block the line to progress on the railways

torpor. We will not allow drastic changes of ownership to be forced upon industries on no evidence except a political theory and with no practical regard to the results they may bring. To us the tests will always be — what will conduce most to efficiency, and what will render the greatest service to the community . . .'

Labour won the 1945 election. The railways were nationalized. So too was much of the road haulage industry. Many bus services were already municipally owned. The leftward trend in public transport was in the ascendancy. Railway nationalization was a 'political', not a 'transport', proposition. Whether this was a successful implementation of a 'political theory' or a policy to 'conduce most to efficiency' and to 'render the greatest service to the community' is a matter of opinion.

The 1948 structure was subsequently amended by the 1953 Transport Act. Those five post-war years had been inadequate in planning, carrying through and assessing such fundamental changes as were inherent — or should have been — in the act of nationalization. In 1953 the British Transport Commission itself took over the responsibilities of the Railway Executive that had run the railways from 1947, then the BTC was itself abolished by the 1962 Transport Act. It is not difficult to make the case that the integration of transport services envisaged in the 1947 Act never had a chance to prove its viability or otherwise.

What is a matter of fact is that, from nationalization in 1948, the nation saw railway operating profits steadily erode and, by 1955, disappear (by 1961 the annual loss on BR had risen to £86.9 million). That

As steam's reign on the Great Western Railway approached its nadir, long hours were spent in silent vigil in Sonning Cutting. 'Castles' on the Worcester and Hereford expresses, or 'Halls' and '61xx' tanks were the height of our hopes. On 2 November 1963 it would therefore have seemed to be unlikely as I took this photograph of a 'Warship' diesel-hydraulic on a down West of England express, that such a shot could be of any interest. Note my umbrella getting itself into the picture; another sign of the times, when golf umbrellas were restricted to golf-courses.

Naturally, the distinctive nature of the choice of diesel-hydraulic power by the Western Region was, like Brunel's broad gauge, rejected under the weight of pressure from the (continued on page 35)

year — 1955 — saw the publication of the Modernisation Plan, with its proposed substitution of electric and diesel haulage for steam, plus resignalling and other forms of modernization designed to return the railways to profitability. The modernization programme did not, however, take into account the larger social and economic factors at the time. By 1960 it had become obvious that the Plan had failed, and the problems of the railways could only escalate unless a programme of rationalization was undertaken. Prime Minister Harold Macmillan, speaking in the House of Commons on 10 March 1960, said: 'First the industry must be of a size and pattern suited to modern conditions and prospects. In particular, the railway system must be remodelled to meet current needs, and the modernization plan adapted to this new shape.'

Thus, in due course, came Dr Beeching. Appointed in 1961, there eventually appeared, in March 1963, 'The Reshaping of British Railways'. For a task of such importance, not just for the railways but for the nation, one can be excused perhaps for being surprised at the document's brevity. In a mere 60 pages is analysed the existing state and future prospects of the passenger, freight and parcels services of the railways, and from that analysis were drawn conclusions, the implementation of which has had, and still does have, a fundamental effect on public transport in Britain.

It is tempting to quote great chunks of this document, but one sentence, in the Foreword, seems to sum up the problem thus: '. . . there had never before been any systematic assembly of a basis of information upon which planning could be founded'. In addition, and of essential importance if the nation's rail transport system is to be more than a dogmatic football kicked from one end of the political spectrum to the other, is the acknowledgement that 'individual convenience and total social benefit are not necessarily compatible, and that competing forms of transport cannot be costed on strictly comparable bases.'

One important issue settled at that time was this 'social service' aspect of the provision of railway services. The 1962 Act stated that it was the duty of the Railways Board to provide services as seemed expedient, having regard to efficiency and economy. However, the Transport Select Committee had previously recommended that specific uneconomic services, which may have to be continued for social reasons, should be given specific subsidies. This was rejected by the then Government because, according to A.J. Pearson in his book *Railways and the Nation*, 'it was considered it would be difficult to isolate and assess the loss of particular services, and some services unprofitable at one time might become profitable later'. The eventual crystallization of the notion of social obligation for the railways became encapsulated by Sir Peter Parker who, as Chairman of the British Railways Board from 1976 to 1983, coined the phrase 'the social railway', as distinct from 'the commercial railway'.

Perhaps the most important aspect not dealt with by the report was the question of what effort was to be made on marketing the railway more effectively, on assessing customer demand and matching it with service supply. Also, what plans were to be considered, *vide* the 1930s 'Fair Deal for the Railways', to mount a political campaign to seek to ensure that rail's competitors were to be made to bear a fairer share of the costs they incurred and which are funded out of general taxation rather than their revenue generated? In a nutshell, how was the 'financial' column of Beeching to be set alongside the 'social', the 'economic' or the 'political' columns of what is — or what should have been — a major socio-economic document studying public transport requirement, potential and operation for a generation?

Assessed cost of operating a public transport service by rail, rather than by taxpayer-funded road, can be seen to be unequal in numerous ways, not considered by Beeching. Let us take rates. Railways have always traditionally paid 'rates'. In 1909, A.D. Lomas, Assistant Land and Rating Surveyor of the Lancashire & Yorkshire Railway, set down the methods by which he sought to 'value' the railway for rating purposes. It was necessary to divide the L & Y into two parts, namely Directly Productive (the line) and Indirectly Productive (stations, etc). Thereafter it was usual, he says, 'to consider two persons, the landlord and the hypothetical tenant'. In dealing with the first category, he writes:

'First ascertain the gross receipts by taking out the train mileage and applying the earnings per train mile; or, by going to a very

(continued from page 34)
'conformists' on British Railways. At least it makes this photograph of some interest.

The first five 'Warship' Class, Numbers D600-604, were built by Western Region in 1958, the D800 Class thereafter totalling 71 in all. The original colour scheme was Brunswick green with a single blue-grey stripe along the bodyside between the cab doors, as seen here but without the yellow panel. Excepting bogie troubles, duly rectified, the D800s gave good service; but they were, in BR terms, non-standard, and had to go. All 71 had disappeared from service by the end of 1972.

The late Lord Beeching: appointed by Marples; approved by Macmillan; roundly cursed; richly praised; rarely ignored. (Redland plc)

heavy expense, take out the receipts from the company's books
in mileage proportion; measure the geographical length in the
township or parish, and multiply the receipts by such length to
get the earnings in the parish.'

That is but the beginning. Merely as a means of illustrating the historic
burden borne by the railways — for historic reasons totally unrelated
to an era when they must compete with (deregulated) road competition — I list the items he had to include in his schedule of Tenants'
Capital:

'Locomotives
Passenger-train vehicles
Goods-train vehicles
Stores
Tools and machinery: Locomotives and C & W Departments
Movable tools — Telegraph department
Movable tools — Hydraulic department
Movable tools — Stores department
Breakdown appliances — Locomotive department
Portable cranes — Traffic and permanent-way departments
Working drawings — Locomotives and C & W departments
Patterns — Locomotive departments
Telegraph apparatus
Office and Station furniture (including barrows, chains, timetable-
boards, etc)
Uniforms
Books and stationery
Wagon sheets, etc
Horses and harness (for shunting)
Sacks
Guards' and brakemen's watches
Ropes
Floating capital'

Blithely, he adds later, 'We are now in a position to make a rating valu-
ation', etc, etc. From this historic base is assessed the Uniform Business Rate, as a replacement to the rating system, to be paid by British
Rail, while the competing coaches park in the street, causing traffic
congestion and pollution rather than pay for the space they occupy.
As Mr W.C. Ryde KC, arbitrating in the Salford Case in 1905, stated,
'. . . terminals must be regarded as part of the indivisible sum paid for
carriage of a consignment of goods between two places, and must be
regarded as earned by the line between those two places; it follows that
the service of carriage must be regarded as beginning not later than

the time when the goods are loaded in the railway wagon, and ending when they are unloaded or handed over by the railway company, and that the line over which the goods travel from beginning to end of the journey must be regarded as directly productive of the sum paid to the company for the carriage of these goods. . .' Herein lies yet another historic distortion in the means of assessing costs of road versus rail *public* transport.

In 1899, the total Gross Estimated Rental of Rateable Hereditaments for England and Wales was £211,449,918; of this, the total Gross Estimated Rental of Railways, including stations and depots, was £20,103,154. That was 90 years ago; they have been paying ever since, albeit with a reduced burden. Who says the railways make no net contribution to the nation?

The replacement of the rating system by the Community Charge could have provided the Government with an opportunity to eliminate one of the anomalous distortions of rail versus road costs, by exempting British Rail from this liability. What a forlorn hope!

In answer to a Parliamentary Question, the Local Government Minister, David Hunt, told me on 15 November 1989 in relation to the Community Charge that 'British Rail's rate bill for property assessed on this basis in England in 1990/91 would be about £57.5 million'. Naturally, coaches in London will continue to park in the streets, paying

Introduced in 1962, when in September of that year the first member of the class, D1500, emerged from the Brush locomotive works at Loughborough for handing over to BR, the Type 4 has, since then, become the 'Black Five' of the diesel era, handling almost all traffic with facility.

Here, in two-tone green livery, an early member of the class wheels an excursion train off the Windsor branch at Slough, via the now-lifted west curve to the GW down main line, in June 1964. Lifting spurs like this saved a few pounds, yet now preclude such traffic gaining direct rail access to Windsor from the West Country, Oxford, Birmingham, etc; typical of the short-sighted, penny-pinching policies forced on BR by a road-orientated transport policy.

Hardly the most exciting photograph I took at Old Oak Common, but, in its colour scheme, one of the least common. D1733, seen here on 5 July 1964, was temporarily painted thus for hauling the XP64 experimental train set, although the orange panel was soon removed. Note the 81A shed-plate underneath the panel with the then new BR logo.

nothing so to do, but creating congestion, wasting police time and polluting the air.

* * *

Where, however, does foresight end and hindsight begin? Would it have been possible to envisage the effect of the motorway-building programme on the travel patterns of commerce and industry? Was there an extrapolation of the effects of the steady change from a manufacturing to a service based economy into the future years covered by the Report? What thought was given to the effect of increasing car-ownership and its resultant congestion on the attractions of travel by rail? What assumptions were made about technological improvement, increased speed and its effect on the competitiveness of rail travel versus its competitors? What detailed discussions took place about the need for, and the effect of, improved productivity on the costs of providing rail services?

'The Reshaping of British Railways' failed to tackle any of these vital questions in any depth — or at all. Produced at the behest of a Minister of Transport in a Conservative Government, its overriding priority was to tackle the mounting financial deficit. It was a fact that the 17,800 route miles in this vast system existing in 1962, with 7,000 stations, 474,538 staff, 12,657 locomotives, 11,032 multiple unit vehicles, 35,057 coaches and parcels vans and the phenomenal total of 848,591 wagons, were a legacy of history: a history born of more than a century of governmental diktat exacerbated by war. To start from this point, as though it was the result of a failed business plan rather than an historic legacy, was to ensure that the railways had no chance of making a fresh start. That the remit, and the character, of the man charged with the task of correcting the situation, one Dr Beeching, was dedicated more to damage limitation than to adventurous creation, *vide* his view about the Crewe-Glasgow electrification of the West Coast Main Line, combined with the ministerial brief which confined his job description, perhaps made the outcome inevitable. The 'Reshaping' saw the railway still on the defensive. It was the politicians who made the rules, whilst the railwaymen took the blame.

Only now, in the 1990s, is the tide turning, yet there are many who still do not appreciate the position, and the new belief in the vital environmental role of the railway system has arrived too late to save numerous services, lines and stations that need a railway. Beeching did more than close railway lines: he affected attitudes to the railway which, unfairly and unfortunately, persist to this day.

In truth, neither Beeching nor British Railways initiated the policy of railway closure: in my constituency the line from Christchurch to Ringwood succumbed as long ago as 1935. This area of growth, now pregnant with the ambitions of the developers, was described by Mr George Wingfield-Digby in the November 1935 *Railway Magazine* thus: 'It traverses a wonderful area of (still) wild and boggy moorland between Christchurch and Hurn, and a delightful district of undulating pinewood parkland between Hurn and Ringwood.' He concludes thus: 'The small station of Hurn is far from any habitation, except the railwayman's cottage. It has two platforms, but the eastern one has been dismantled for many years and the track serving it taken up.' It is hard to recognize this area today, from this description.

There was, however, all the difference in the world between an isolated closure as at Hurn and the Beeching formula of mass decimation. Beeching's plans inevitably caused commercial and industrial users of the railway to doubt its long-term future. Pearson quotes the reaction of the Chief Transport Officer of the Metal Box Company to 'The Reshaping of British Railways'. He stated, 'It would seem that, since it is apparently the Government's intention to secure the development of the railways as a normal commercial enterprise and treated as such by the public and industry, our railway system will be made to shrink until only a limited number of profitable trunk and branch lines and special facilities remain.'

Beeching's remit was political: economic rather than social, or even national, transport considerations were paramount. Richard Hardy, as a Beeching supporter, allows to be said on the jacket of his book: 'Thus rather than the "axeman" epithet, he deserves recognition as the preserver of Britain's railway network'. Yet within the book Hardy, with his inside knowledge, highlights fundamental flaws, none more revealing than his comment on page 61: 'Beeching did not draw his general managers extensively or regularly into central policy making, preferring, as has previously been shown, to work through a small circle of tried and trusted people. But whereas his teams in ICI were made up of men of considerable experience in that industry, few members of the original Board could show themselves to be tried and trusted in the railway business. And so we must now return to the fascinating composition of his Board, and try to decide whether the mistakes that Beeching made, if he in fact did so, justify the oft-quoted remark that despite his greatness in every other field, he lacked the ability to choose the right men to support him throughout his four years as Chairman.'

Few would dispute that Beeching had a brilliant mind. Equally — with beneficial hindsight — his terms of reference, drawn up by Ernest Marples, were to blame for his 'axeman' image. According to Hardy's words just quoted, he seriously misjudged the importance of the advice of experienced railwaymen in determining his conclusions. To these two features add the impact of his Report on British industry, as quoted by the Chief Transport Officer of the Metal Box Company, and you have the ingredients to decide on a suitable epithet for a man whose name still means so much.

2
ON THE BOARD

Some people prefer to travel by train. For others, speed of journey dictates their mode of travel. Inadequate alternatives and/or congestion dictate travel patterns. Yet in a modern industrial state, the creation or solution of these problems is usually in the hands of the Government. Investment criteria, the relative values of convenience versus environment or the claims of the competing spending Departments of State, determined in the annual Ministerial confrontation with the Treasury, determine the outcome. It is probably true to generalize by stating that those who favour the highest all-round levels of public expenditure tend to support the genre of Government which, historically, coincides when in office with the least productive economic performance. Inevitably, as a politician, my contribution to thinking on this matter, in writing this book, caused me to wonder who might best have something original to say on this subject. One man has, uniquely, been both Minister of Transport and Chairman of the British Railways Board.

Son of a railwayman, Richard Marsh, now Lord Marsh, was elected as Labour MP for Greenwich in 1959. His obvious natural ability soon brought him to the attention of the Labour Whips' office, and in due course Prime Minister Harold Wilson brought him into Government as Parliamentary Under Secretary at the Ministry of Labour, and thereafter at the Ministry of Technology. (Those of you who remember the election of the first Wilson Government in 1964 may recall phrases such as 'the white heat of the technological revolution'.) Dick Marsh was, and is, a pragmatist. He is also a most agreeable man, and readily consented to allow me to interview him for this book.

In 1974, Heath was out and Wilson was back. Dick Marsh returned to Government, climbing up the ladder, serving in the Ministry of Power, dealing with coal, North Sea oil and other energy industries. He then became Minister of Transport.

'Frankly, I was not terribly interested in the politics, but in the whole management scene of these "industrial" ministries. I worked closely with industrialists, but was often in conflict with the politicians, particularly Barbara Castle. She was an amazing woman — 100 per cent political — but a disaster as a Minister in an industrial department.

The Rt Hon the Lord Marsh of Mannington, the only man to have been both Minister of Transport and Chairman of British Rail. (UPPA Ltd)

'The necessary railway': Euston, on 1 March 1963, still provides the backdrop for clean locomotives going about their business. The LMS Stanier 'Black Five' 4-6-0 can justifiably claim to be amongst the most versatile and reliable locomotives ever designed; 842 members of the class were built between 1935 and 1951. One of them was No 45198, allocated at this date to Willesden MPD, and seen here still adorned with BR's 'lion and wheel' emblem.

Barbara Castle epitomized the problem of politicians running a business. I fell out with her in Cabinet Committee, particularly over the Steel Corporation and the Transport Act and the London Transport Act.

'We were doctrinally completely opposed and the question of the Humber Bridge probably epitomizes the two different approaches; for years there had been talk about building a bridge across the Humber in order to bring business into the less prosperous parts of the region. What nobody considered was that it would also take business/prosperity *out* again. No one looked carefully at the commercial implications and Barbara Castle gave the commitment for the bridge to be built at a public meeting during a by-election. It is an example of public money being wasted because a political rather than a business decision was taken. The same applied to Bristol West Dock.

'By the time I arrived at British Rail, Beeching had produced his report and there was no evidence at all that the massive butchery of the railways had fundamentally changed the financial position of BR. The Chief Executive of BR at that time was David Bowick, who had been Secretary to the Beeching Committee and was therefore firmly convinced that if you identified the loss-makers and closed them down you would be all right. One of the problems always was that there were Cabinet Ministers who were violently anti-railway, particularly Tony Crosland. They regarded investment in passenger transport as a regressive form of taxation. As far as they were concerned, the Intercity services were used by business people and the commuter services in and out of London were used by the middle-class, so that they regarded them as a total waste of money.

'I believe Beeching was fundamentally wrong, and told him so on many occasions. His whole plan was based on the misconception that the financial problems of the railways could be eradicated by identifying the loss-making services and closing them. The difficulty, of course, is that it is not a straightforward matter to identify loss-making services and cut them out, since in many cases profit-making services are dependent upon loss-making feeder services and the cost of closing down lines can be much higher than the benefits. Indeed, this point is implicitly recognized in West Germany, where the Federal Government pays 'only' 90 per cent of the losses on the suburban services, as these services themselves act as feeders for the profitable InterCity routes.

'When I was at BR we tried to identify the "necessary" railway. We did that by taking the whole network and "breaking off" the unprofitable bits. On that basis you were left with a core, of commuter services, East Coast Main Line, Intercity in and out of London, which showed that to talk in terms simply of cutting off the loss-making bits is not even to understand the structure. A lot of the infrastructure, for example, is in the wrong place because of demographic changes, and the transitional cost of changing this would be astronomical; it would, for example, include the cost of moving main line stations to different locations. [These comments bear out the view that in time of war or emergency, now-closed lines could be sorely missed.]

'John Peyton, when he was Minister, had a very clear attitude and made clear decisions. Tony Crosland, as I have said, was hostile to the railways and on the only occasion he came to BR to see a presentation, ostentatiously fell asleep! He was not even faintly interested. The senior Civil Servants were anti-railways, as were the Treasury.'

I asked him if he thought that our whole political system, with changes of Government and short-term financial planning, militated against sensible long-term planning of railway policy.

'Having had experience of both Governments' interfering,' he replied, 'I have to say that Edward Heath was the person who intervened to a fantastic extent. If you think of politicians as a non-executive board, they are totally unused to performing an executive role and their objectives are different from a board appointed to run a business. A Minister cannot take an interest in all the businesses for which he is responsible; they are too big and too complex. If you think about the Minister of Transport, he has to think about the Inland Waterways Board, the entire road system, the whole question of vehicle safety, the National

Freight Corporation, BR, the airlines, etc. BR itself had several different businesses to run — hotels, property, transport police, ferries, hovercraft. The amount of involvement that a Minister can have in one thing is negligible.

'When I was Minister, there had been 25 Ministers in 50 years. You cannot get involved in the running of the business. Politics is basically short-term and the politician's objectives are short-term; there is no planning beyond the next general election. This means that the whole timescale is totally short-term and the objectives are wrong. If I ask a merchant bank to act for a company, I expect them to advise me on the details of that company; I don't want to hear what is going to happen to the balance of payments, or whether the line the company is proposing to take is going to cause unemployment. But with politicians, the success of the business is very far down their list of priorities. They are concerned with the effects on their constituencies (Richard Hardy, in *Beeching, Champion of the Railways?*, recalls how Ernest Marples saved the Liverpool-Southport and Ormskirk services, but he is too polite to mention that Marples represented a Merseyside constituency); the effect on the balance of payments; the effect on the Treasury and on taxation. If you think of the Cabinet as a merchant bank, who know nothing about your business and the way it should be run, but who think they do, you begin to see the problem of Ministerial intervention.

'The Treasury probably has more capability for planning, but its objectives are the problem. I think that cuts in investment illustrate this point well: politicians will always cut investment because the effect is long-term. You can cut vast sums and no one will realize. When I was at BR and John Peyton was Minister, we were asked to cut investment. At the time we were replacing short-welded track with long-welded track, which is much cheaper to maintain. As investment cuts became greater and greater, we reached the point where we had cut all we could, but were still 2 per cent short of target — which I seem to recall in 1975 was 15 per cent. One possibility which was discussed was to stop the rebuilding programme at London Bridge Station, but this was rejected. I then had a meeting with John Peyton and, of course, his Civil Servants. I explained the situation to the Minister and told him that we could not find a further 2 per cent to cut. But his Civil Servant referred to the programme to replace short-rail track with long-welded and pointed out that there was a sizeable amount in the budget for that. I said that we were only replacing short-rail with long-welded where it was actually worn out. But, said the Civil Servant, if you replace short-rail with short-rail, that is revenue account; if you replace short-rail with long-welded, that is capital investment. In other words, he was advocating that we should take a course of action that would, in the long term, be more expensive, in order to make the necessary cuts in investment! John Peyton went to the Treasury and we were finally allowed to continue with the long-welded programme.'

Opposite *Even into the last year of steam on BR, the sight of a Stanier LMS '8F' 2-8-0 was quite common — if you knew where to go. Pushed back into an ever smaller corner of the country, the North-West was steam's final stronghold and Speke Junction Shed (8C), to the south-east of Liverpool, was one of those that survived into 1968, steam's final year.*

Opened comparatively late by the LNWR, in May 1886, it was a large 12-road depot designed to accommodate 60 locomotives. It started life, and remained, dedicated to freight work. Thus, by the end of steam, '8Fs' and 'Black Fives' comprised virtually the entire allocation.

With the coal stage behind, and the electrified line to Lime Street to the right, '8F' No 48060, a Speke Junction engine built in 1936 by Vulcan Foundry, moves away from the coal stage having replenished supplies on 10 August 1967. Her shedplate has gone, replaced by a painted substitute. Such a familiar sight will never die in the memory of those of us who saw it so often.

Whilst the French poured millions into the TGV and built a new railway for it, our engineers saw a brilliant project starved to death. The Advanced Passenger Train (APT) could run at 150 mph on the conventional railway of Locke and Stephenson. Lacking financial commitment, it withered and died. Here, in October 1984, with my wife Jane in the cab, unit No 370007 prepares to leave Euston on a special high-speed run to Glasgow. On each leg of the journey we ran way ahead of schedule, with resultant lengthy stops en route to await our path. Few projects better epitomize our failure to back potential success.

Doubtless numerous similar examples can be cited. The temptation for Government to intervene in the day-to-day activities of the nationalized industries has tended to militate against the ability of management to manage. The relationship works best when Government resists temptation, be it in industrial relations or, for example, purchasing policy. Erstwhile Labour MP Richard Marsh, describing himself now as 'somewhat to the right of Gengis Khan', has no hesitation in praising Mrs Thatcher for her non-interference in the daily business of running the nationalized industries. That is not to say that she lacks the will or vision to give their leaders clear guidelines; but she leaves it to them to achieve the targets set by the Government of the day.

On the other hand, Marsh's own experience as Chairman of BR leads him, as we have already seen, to catalogue Edward Heath as 'probably the most interventionist'. He told me, 'I recall at the time of the Advanced Passenger Train, BR had to buy a thyristor control system for it. We were looking at the equipment produced by ASEA of Sweden, which was already in service, but Arnold Weinstock wanted us to order from GEC. He went to see Heath, who summoned me. I told him that BR had enough problems with the APT without providing a test-bed for untried equipment. I pointed out that it is a very complex vehicle and that it was absolutely crucial to have the right control system and that we were faced with the choice between one which was tried and tested and the other which had not been. He asked me "how our companies could ever export if nationalized industries bought from our competitors", and asked me if I had no responsibility in the matter. I said "not as far as GEC's sales policies are concerned." Heath was very angry.

'There is no doubt that Ministerial intervention causes many problems, particularly in industrial relations, again something in which the Prime Minister does not intervene. But at the time of the Heath Government, if you had a strike on the railway, you had Jim Prior at the Ministry of Employment on the phone constantly. The level of intervention was colossal. I well remember being at home ill in bed and Maurice Macmillan turning up late one night. He had been for a drink with Vic Feather and told him that they could not intervene if the Board remained intransigent. Because of the intervention, the dispute was settled the next day at a higher price than was needed.'

Where modern motive power scores. On a foul, wet day, 6 June 1964, three steam engines — each with driver and fireman — fall back from the train they have just assisted up the Lickey Incline. '94xx' 0-6-0 pannier tanks Nos 8402 and 9493, plus '9F' 2-10-0 No 92230, have helped to shove a freight, hauled by GWR 'Hall' 4-6-0 No 5984 Linden Hall — also with driver and fireman — up the 1 in 37 incline from Bromsgrove, on the Bristol-Birmingham main line. Here, at Blackwell, they will cross over from the 'up' to the 'down' line and run back to
(continued overleaf)

(continued from page 47)
Bromsgrove to await their next turn of duty.

Impressive and exciting it may have been to watch, even on such an awful day: economic it certainly was not. Modern diesel and, even more so electric traction render such shows of physical muscle-power unnecessary.

The Rt Hon the Lord Peyton of Yeovil, former Minister of Transport: a man not afraid to speak his mind.

Nothing in this interview reduced the impression that the answer to the question 'Who needs a railway?' is political as well as economic. During my early years in the House of Commons, Messrs (now Lords) Marsh and Peyton had, of course, sat on opposite sides of the House. It would be interesting to see how time and experience had affected their views.

Where Dick Marsh responded with alacrity and in detail, John Peyton seemed less accustomed to contemplating questions on his years in charge of the nation's transport. In response to my initial question, 'Was Beeching right?', John Peyton pondered before answering.

'This is very difficult to judge. Looking back at it, the real problem was that the railways were in a very battered and exhausted state after the war, during which they had performed a very vital task, but no investment of any sort had been made. Then at the very worst possible moment, they were taken over by the Government. From that time on, of course, they had to contend with the Treasury for money and the Treasury is more interested in the nation's cash flow than it is in the problems of any particular industry.

'The railways also suffered from the fact that there were a lot of enthusiasts who resisted the closure of any line. There are lines — or there were in my day — where it would be better to give the passengers the money and supply them with free petrol and tell them to make their own arrangements, rather than keep an under-used railway line open. I don't know that Beeching had a very fundamental impact. It was necessary to have some kind of business judgement on the railways. Alf Robens did something different in coal; he was sufficient of a politician to understand how to deal with the Government machine. The Government machine, although it has many people who are intelligent, perceptive, erudite, and so forth, nevertheless has a total character which is slow-moving, cowardly and incompetent.'

It is interesting to note how much emphasis John Peyton places upon the character of the people involved; not only the BR Chairmen, but also the Chairmen of other nationalized industries with whom he came into contact during his ministerial career. His comments on Alf Robens and Dennis Rooke, in relation to 'their' industries, was made in perhaps critical comparison with recent top management in other industries, such as rail and electricity. Yet he certainly made clear his view that the best Chairmen of our nationalized industries are those who are willing to challenge, if necessary, the views of their political masters. In response to my proposition that it is in the nature and tradition of our system that this is not the way such men have traditionally behaved, he responded: 'There is such a thing as resignation'.

We also discussed BR's current response to the challenge of the Channel Tunnel. His words were: 'BR needs to get some decent managers and give them the chance to manage. The Channel Tunnel offers them long-haul opportunities, but much of their management is sloppy and there is no justification for the present system. They won't make the

issues clear. Let us have some plain speaking. The most important thing now seems to be not to make anyone feel uncomfortable. People don't say things out loud.'

As with Dick Marsh, and seemingly as a permanent feature of political debate *vis-à-vis* public policy, national interest and the nationalized industries, the Treasury loomed large in John Peyton's mind as the source of aggravation. 'The Treasury is very difficult to get to grips with. No one ever has a right to see the Treasury. In a Department you can see the Departmental Minister, but the Treasury won't allow you to see the Chief Secretary.'

When I mentioned Dick Marsh's views about the predominance of short-term considerations in Treasury thinking, John Peyton agreed, adding, 'Yes, that's one of the great handicaps of the system. If you have a business, you have to watch interest rates. You may slow down, but you don't stop really profitable investment. But the problems for the Treasury in dealing with the nation's cash flow are very different. I made the decision (Fred Mulley claimed it was him, but it was me!)

'The line to Crewe had already been electrified, but the Treasury was against electrification north of Crewe, which meant a change of locomotive at Crewe' (Lord Peyton). On 6 March 1965 when I took this photograph, steam, diesel and electric power co-existed at Crewe. Although a little scratched, this shot of Stanier 'Black Five' No 44679, with 5A Crewe North shedplate, emerging under the wires through the fog, perhaps typifies that era for BR. The locomotive — one of the class with Skefko roller-bearings — was engaged on station pilot (continued overleaf).

(continued from page 49)
work and was joining the Liverpool and Manchester sections of a southbound train which would be taken forward by electric haulage.

The railwayman, left, seems today to epitomize 'times past'.

as to whether the line north of Crewe up to Glasgow should be electrified. The Treasury argued against it. The line to Crewe had already been electrified, but the Treasury was against electrification north of Crewe, which meant, of course, a change of locomotive at Crewe.'

To those of us privileged to have seen John Peyton at close range, even to have been at the sharp end of his spiky responses, it came as no surprise to find him both pungent in pinpointing weakness in any argument, yet original in his analyses of problems. He highlighted the discrepancies between support for the conventional and mediocre, but disfavour for the unconventional and innovative. Commenting on the role of the Civil Service and its response to the eternal 'road v rail' discussion within his Department, he said, 'Nothing really ever changed. It was a sort of game. There was a pattern; you played the game along with everybody else.' He reminisced: 'Peter Parker told me that when BRB moved from Marylebone to Euston, there were little groups who had lunched together for donkey's years. But when they were moved to Euston to open-plan offices, they all rushed for partitions and walls.

'I remember visiting Bristol Parkway with Dick Marsh. He said, "Your Department won't allow us to have signs on the motorway to Parkway Station." I said they *were* to be put up; and a few months later I asked my officials, "Has anything been done about those signs." The answer was no, "because only signs to airports are put on motorways." I told them to put the signs up, as they had been asked in the first place. I received tear-stained minutes about all this! Later Dick Marsh thanked me for the signs and gave me a chit for £500 he had been sent for the signs. He asked me what to do with it. I told him "Put it anywhere you like, as long as you don't pay it!"'

3
ROADS AND TRACKS

This is a railway book, but the influence of railways on our society can neither be studied nor assessed without a passing glance at the modes of transport that preceded and succeeded the invention of the railway. Trade, rather than social mobility, has been man's main motivation for travel, as witness the task for which Britain's earliest 'railroads' were constructed. That the word was 'railroad' is barely surprising, for the inland waterways and the roads were the two main sources of freight mobility. Save for the rivers and canals, therefore, the road 'network' was the main source of national and local transportation.

'From the seaboard of Suffolk and Norfolk, and on the north coast almost to the limits of the great level, stretched a series of swamps, quagmires, small lakes and "broads". . . .from Norwich to Liverpool, and from the mouth of the Ouse at Lynn to the Mersey, where it falls into the Irish Sea, a line of fen, uncultivated moors and morasses stretched across England and separated the northern counties from the midland districts, the old territory of Mercia.' (Rev W. Denton, *England in the Fifteenth Century*, 1888)

It was under conditions such as these that Britain obtained her first roads which were, however, more in the nature of tracks, designed less for the purpose of defence than in the interests of British trade. The mineral wealth and the trading interests which had inspired the routes of the earliest British roads were, side by side with military considerations, leading factors in the particular direction given to the Roman roads that followed them.

Not only were the Roman roads excellently constructed (some of these laid down in Rome and in France have been in use for some 1,500 to 2,000 years), but the broad-minded policy by which the builders themselves were influenced is also a matter of great interest and importance. A network of scientifically designed roads was a part of the Roman plan of campaign; but it was further designed to embrace the existing transport network, and to aid in developing the resources of the country concerned. So the Roman roads, connecting the rising city and commercial centre of London with every part of Britain, were remarkable not only for their artistry, but also because they had been directly

created and controlled by a central authority, a policy invariably opposed by successive States.

With the departure of the Romans, road-making and even road repair were neglected for several centuries. The Roman roads continued to be used, but successive rulers were too busy with wars both at home and abroad to attend to such affairs. The result was that during the Middle Ages the means of internal communication by land was probably worse in Britain than any other country in Western Europe. In these circumstances, the Church took over the task of making or repairing both roads and bridges, the faithful being encouraged to assist in the good work, either through gifts (land, money or even livestock) or by personal labour and with the reward of remission of sins. As well as this, guilds and lay brotherhoods, animated by the religious spirit, were formed in the reign of Richard II for the repair of roads and bridges. The situation at this period is summed up by stating that 'the roads in England would have been entirely impassable. . .if the nobility and clergy. . .had not had an immediate and daily interest in possessing passable roads.' (J.J. Jusserand, *English Wayfaring Life in the Middle Ages*, 1891)

There came, however, a period of decline in religious fervour. Less money was given and the clergy became increasingly lax in carrying out their responsibilities. It was not until 1555, well over 1,000 years after the departure of the Romans, that the first general Act was passed, not for the construction but for the repair of roads in this country. That Highway Act created the system of road administration and maintenance which remained the basic framework until the nineteenth century. The Act directed that constables and churchwardens in every parish should 'call together a number of the parochians' and choose two honest persons to serve for a year as surveyors. Besides having responsibility for the 'highway money' (provided by the land-owners) the surveyors had to oversee the parishioners, who each had to work (if able) for four days, of eight hours each, without pay. The surveyor also had to view the roads, highways, watercourses, bridges and pavements three times a year. This principle of compulsory labour was — subject to various modifications — to remain in operation until the passing of the General Highway Act of 1835.

By the seventeenth century, if not earlier, loud complaints were heard. Statute labour failed to provide adequate roads; labourers were said to be lazy and ill-managed; surveyors had no technical skill and neglected their duties. No further general legislation concerning roads was passed until the Restoration, when 'The vast increase of commerce. . .and of the capital city of London. . .brought in such numbers of heavy-wheel carriages as rendered it by degrees impracticable. . .for parishes entirely to keep their own part of the roads in a tolerable condition.' (David Macpherson, *Annals of Commerce*, 1805).

In 1663, there was brought about a system of toll-taking. Macpherson speaks of the system as 'the more equitable and effectual method

Opposite *With the closure of the LNWR line from Chester to Whitchurch, a large chunk of Cheshire is a long way from a railway line. Where once 'Jumbos' and 'Precursors' ran, now Friesians graze, 'twixt Malpas and Broxton.*

In fact, this was a 15-mile rural branch, double-tracked, from Whitchurch to the Chester-Crewe line at Tattenhall Junction. Promoted by the LNWR, it was part of their grand design to deprive the GWR of its monopoly between Shrewsbury and Chester. It was an archetypal example of a 'railway-political' line, although its life was comparatively short, opening in 1872 and closing to passenger traffic, with little fuss, in 1957.

Malpas and Broxton stations lingered on for goods traffic for six years before silently succumbing to the inevitable. With few trains serving few passengers in sparsely populated countryside, this is a line the retention of which would have been hard to plead.

Claims to historic rail-way innovation are legion, but one must surely be the Pen-y-Darren Tramroad. Some 9½ miles long, it ran from Merthyr Tydfil to Navigation House, later known as Abercynon. A plateway on stone blocks, it was built to a gauge of 4ft 2in on a ruling gradient of 1 in 36. Opened in 1802, its unshakeable claim to history revolves around the trials conducted with Richard Trevithick's locomotive in 1804. It is still possible to discern some of the stone blocks of the Tramroad, as seen here.

of tolls, paying at the toll-gates (called turnpikes) by those who use and wear the roads', and this was the view that generally prevailed at that time. It was hoped that the introduction of this Act would save the country from the appalling road conditions. Thus was established the principle of paying for the right to travel, currently being discussed under the jargon of 'privatization'. (It has yet to be seen whether the true cost of motor vehicle usage, such as police time, will be reckoned as an appropriate item for inclusion in cost-assessment.) However, when the adoption of the turnpike system became more general, many people in various parts of the country not only refused to use turnpike roads, or to pay toll if they did use them, but in some cases the toll-gates were destroyed. Will this be a latter-day precedent?

Many contemporary accounts give us an idea as to the bad road conditions. One eighteenth-century traveller, Arthur Young, found the roads 'barbarous and execrable' and describes 'rocky lanes full of huge stones as big as one's horse and abominable holes'. Of the road between Preston and Wigan he remarks: 'I know not in the whole range of language terms sufficiently expressive to describe this infernal road. Let me seriously caution all travellers... to avoid it as they would the devil.'

The growth of foreign trade and manufacturing industries was making the need for proper highways an urgent one. Bad roads seriously hampered the growth of domestic trade. It was frequently cheaper to import European goods into London by sea than to carry similar commodities from the interior of the country on the backs of horses. During the seventeenth and eighteenth centuries, the pack-horse was the almost universal means of carrying goods over land for any distance. Wheeled vehicles were little used on the roads before the seventeenth century. By the reign of James I, large covered road wagons, led by trains of horses, were used as public vehicles, though travel in these crude conveyances was tedious and uncomfortable. Hackney carriages were first used in London from 1634 onwards and post-chaises from 1664, whilst private carriages seem to have come into use at about the same time. The increased use of carts for goods transport seems to have occurred towards the end of the seventeenth and early in the eighteenth century. In London itself, as may be learned from Defoe in his *A Tour through the whole island of Great Britain* (1724), the betterment of the roads around the metropolis led to the citizens flocking out in greater numbers than ever to take lodgings and country houses in 'towns near London'; the beginnings of Greater London and its road network, and the age of the commuter.

Parliament failed to understand the significance of wheeled traffic and produced conflicting regulations concerning the vehicles themselves, the width of the wheels and the number of horses. In the second half of the nineteenth century, methods of road construction improved. It was not, however, improved highways but canals which provided the means of transport that made Britain's industrial revolution possible.

From the earliest times navigable rivers have had very considerable influence on social and economic development. In pre-industrial England they were the principal arteries of commerce, particularly for the long-distance conveyance of heavy goods which could not be moved by pack-horse or wheeled vehicles. By the middle of the eighteenth century, neither improved navigable rivers nor the wretched dirt roads could cater for the transport needs which the growing production and trade of the country imposed on them. New industrial activity was already stirring. While London remained by far the largest centre of population, new areas were beginning to assume importance. Manchester and Liverpool were gradually rising in importance and increasing in population — as were Birmingham and Sheffield. The people in these developing industrial areas needed food, whilst manufacturers required cheap raw materials, fuel and the facilities for marketing their finished products. Fuel was of dominant importance. With the increasing

The role of the Duke of Bridgewater in developing early transport innovations is covered in the adjacent text. Testimony to his influence is recorded on numerous buildings, some great, some less grand, such as the pub in Crewe which illustrated an aqueduct. The sign has been repainted since I photographed it.

demands of the rising industries, the question of coal transport became more and more urgent.

The first industrial canal in England was the Worsley canal, completed in 1761 on the initiative of the third Duke of Bridgewater, and constructed by James Brindley, a remarkable genius and great engineer. The Duke owned coal mines in Worsley, ten miles from Manchester, but due to the expense of both primitive pack-horses and inconvenient river transport, the price of coal at the pit mouth had more than doubled by the time it reached Manchester. The Duke proposed to build a canal and obtained an Act in 1759 for that purpose; it was first used for traffic in 1761, and the coal supply to Manchester subsequently improved and cheapened. Soon the Duke and Brindley were engaged on a larger project to connect the growing port of Liverpool with Manchester. Despite strong opposition — *vide* the proposed Channel Tunnel high-speed rail link — Parliament approved their scheme in 1762, and by 1767 the Bridgewater Canal was a complete success, carrying both freight and passenger traffic and bringing about activity previously unknown in Liverpool and Manchester.

By the time the Bridgewater Canal was completed, another much larger undertaking was being constructed. In 1766, Parliament passed a Bill for the Grand Trunk Canal, a waterway linking the Trent and Mersey. Meanwhile, canals were being authorized in many parts of the country and the era of active canal construction was under way. In less than half a century, a network of canals was woven over Britain.

The financial success of the early canals fired many people with an enthusiasm no less intense than the enthusiasm for railways half a century later. In 1789, a boom in canal development began and the 'canal mania' reached its peak in 1792-3, when many ill-founded schemes were put forward and speculation in canal shares was rife. In the years 1791 to 1794 no fewer than 81 canal and other navigational Acts were passed. The boom was over by 1797, causing losses for many who had been caught up in the speculative fever; some projected canals were never built and others were abandoned uncompleted.

Unfortunately, the enterprise and service of many canal carriers declined once they had established themselves as going concerns. Complaints were made about delays and the inconsistency of carriers' fees. The monopolistic position of some undertakings was a source of public resentment. Perhaps the greatest defect of canals was the lack of uniformity in structure, which neither engineers nor the Government had done anything to supervise. The variety of differences in length, width and depth of locks frustrated the development of through traffic, and also discouraged, with a few notable exceptions, improvements in the size, type and construction of canal boats. Market factors alone were inadequate regulators of public transport, even in these early years. These deficiencies in canal construction and operation were to prove a decisive weakness in the era of railway competition, which began in the second quarter of the nineteenth century, although they do not detract from the immense social and economic advantages which canals brought to Britain in the late eighteenth and early nineteenth centuries.

The first railways were built, like the canals some 60 years earlier, because of the need for cheaper, better and more reliable transport than existing facilities could provide. It was exasperation with the road and canal networks that first induced manufacturers and others to risk money in railway development (just as exasperation with the railways, a hundred years later, drove traders into sending their goods by road). The existence of this demand was not enough solely to ensure the construction of railways. Their success in the second quarter of the nineteenth century depended on at least two other factors, namely the production of suitable rails for the special track, and the perfecting of a steam locomotive that could run on rails. The special track was no nineteenth century development, but had its origins at least two centuries earlier in the old tramways and 'plate-ways' of the mineral and colliery lines, horse-drawn routes often connecting mineral workings with the adjacent coastline. By the end of the seventeenth century, wooden tramways were fairly common in mining areas and were improved by the fixing of wrought iron plates to the wooden rails to form 'plate-ways'. This was the model for subsequent railway practice. Experiments with wrought iron rails were taking place before the end of the eighteenth century, but were not very successful. Cast iron rails were therefore used, but, as both Trevithick and Stephenson discovered in early experiments with steam locomotives, they were too brittle for heavy weights and high speeds. Ultimately, after further experiments, John Birkinshaw, of Bedlington Ironworks, patented in 1820 a method of rolling wrought iron bars into a shape similar to the cast iron rail. The Bedlington-type rails had the advantage of durability, and wrought iron rails soon supplanted all other types.

It was the supersession of horse traction by the steam locomotive that gave the railway its decisive advantage over the canal. The credit for the first successful demonstration of steam haulage belongs to George Stephenson, although his achievement was only made possible by the experiments of many others before him. The developers of the railway from Swansea to Mumbles, for example, would never accept the predominance attributed by history to the Stephensons in railway matters.

Most of the railways of Great Britain grew up in piecemeal and haphazard fashion, often in short, unconnected lengths up and down the country. Parliament adopted an initially sloppy approach to the idea of a national plan for the railways, even allowing two different gauges to develop. Had there been a thorough investigation, impartially undertaken, into the relative merits of Brunel's 'broad' gauge and the 'narrow' gauge that eventually won the battle, railway history might have been very different. Whilst, however, Parliament itself remained nervous of interference with private enterprise, the railways were beginning to possess much monopoly power, and some people were ready, even in the 1830s, to criticise the freedom that the railways were being allowed. This opposition and the consequent high capital cost this imposed on the companies, was an important factor in the early development of Britain's railways. Such history must not be forgotten as a similar debate gets under way today, although it is the public good rather than the landowners' private interests that requires a response from Government.

The construction of the main bulk of the British railway system was largely the result of promotion undertaken in two bursts of speculative activity, from 1836 to 1837 and from 1845 to 1847. The two railway manias increased the mileage of lines open for traffic from about 500 in 1838 to about 4,600 a decade later. The significance of the railway mania of the mid-1840s for British railway development was twofold. Firstly, it resulted in the completion of the main trunk of the modern railway system. Secondly, it witnessed the first substantial railway amalgamations in Britain and made Parliament increasingly concerned about the growth of the monopoly power of the larger companies. Although there had been minor amalgamations previously, the movement really started in 1844, the great consolidation of the year being the creation of the Midland Railway. In 1845 there were three railway amalgamations, and the London & North Western Railway added, by subsequent amalgamations and purchases, 1,000 miles to its system between 1846 and 1870 alone. After 1847, the consolidation movement died down, the amalgamations of these years having largely impressed on the British railway system its future pattern. Indeed, today's railway map is clearly discernible from these developments. Unlike France, we are not building new railways; if we try, opposition, often mobilized by competitors as in the canal era, is quickly orchestrated. An army of protestors can be assembled at the drop of a hat. Brave local and national leaders become ever more scarce.

During the railway mania, take-over consolidation was carried on amid much speculation and excitement. Some small companies were planned deliberately to be strategically placed to force themselves on powerful neighbours. Such commercial strategies ultimately resulted in a unified railway system emerging from the mass of unco-ordinated lines that had sprung up in every direction. Once the consolidation movement had begun, no company could afford to stand idly by if there was any danger of its rivals securing vital links within its territory. If they failed to take an appropriate opportunity — such as the Great Western's failure to acquire the line between Birmingham and Gloucester — a heavy and long-lasting penalty had to be paid.

By 1850, the main trunk network of the British railway system was pretty well finished, and consolidation of the separate systems had already made substantial headway. A few main routes and many branch and local lines remained to be constructed in the ensuing half century, but the great era of competitive railway projection was drawing to an end. Some sore thumbs stick out, such as the Somerset & Dor-

set Joint Railway's line through the GWR's heartland, but they were the exception rather than the rule. Thus, from the era of railway construction, let us now turn to the era of railway decline.

By visiting various parts of the country, listening to local people's comments on, and reminiscences of, their current railway scene as compared to 25 years ago, and sifting the politically motivated from the practical reality, it becomes clear that some people hanker after the unattainable. To regret the passing of a particular line is one thing; to aver that no lines should ever have been or ever should be closed takes no account of changing habits, available alternatives or specific circumstances.

One of the most poignant moments during the preparation of this book was standing, at track level, at the barred western entrance to Woodhead Tunnel in August 1988. Behind me, towards Manchester, swept the swathe of the former Sheffield, Ashton-under-Lyne & Manchester Railway's line. Latterly part of the Manchester, Sheffield & Lincolnshire, then the Great Central Railway, then the LNER, and finally

In the foreground lies the now-derelict trackbed of the once-electrified Great Central line from Manchester to Sheffield via the new Woodhead Tunnel in the centre of the picture. The juggernauts on the A628 trunk road speak for themselves, mocking our 'transport policy'.

BR, this great trans-Pennine line lay derelict. Was its closure right? Could it have been made into a dedicated freight line? Even if service discontinuance and closure was deemed necessary, should the track formations have been destroyed, thus preventing future reinstatement?

With the growth of trade and traffic generated by the railways themselves, the need for the shortest possible direct link 'twixt the great cities of Sheffield and Manchester was — and is — self-evident. Traffic growth caused the Great Central Railway to discuss electrification of the Woodhead line, as the route has always been known. In 1926 the LNER produced detailed proposals for electrification of this busy line, their scheme intending simultaneously to reduce operating costs and to increase line capacity by 50 per cent. With the economic difficulties of 1929, electrification was not started until 1936. Work was interrupted by the Second World War but resumed in 1946. Far from these 20 years

(1926-46), with the rapid development of road traffic, causing any thought of abandonment, it was decided that the traffic potential remained so great that the significant decision was taken to build a brand new, double-track Woodhead Tunnel to replace the two original bores. Authorized in 1947 under the LNER Development Programme, work began in February 1949. With a workforce of 1,000 men, and living conditions unrecognizable from those faced by the army of navvies who built the original bores a century earlier, the new Woodhead Tunnel was opened to electric-hauled trains in 1954.

I contemplated all this as, standing 'twixt the derelict platforms of the erstwhile Woodhead Station, an unending stream of juggernauts trundled over the head of the closed tunnel on the A628 road across the Pennines. Notwithstanding completion of the M62 motorway from Manchester to West Yorkshire, there clearly remains very heavy road traffic willing to forgo motorway travel for the shorter but crowded, narrow and tortuous trans-Pennine routes, such as the A628 and A57. In spite of this, BR closed its most up-to-date rail link between Manchester and Sheffield. Whilst realizing that the 1,500 volt dc system was to be superseded by the decision to concentrate BR main line electrification on 25,000 volts ac, the Woodhead line could have been converted when its dc system became life-expired; yet it was not to be. Whilst the demise of Woodhead had much to do with the decline in the very coal traffic for which it was electrified, those juggernauts crossing the Pennines surely point to the foolishness of not keeping options open in order to be able to take advantage over the years of changes in traffic patterns.

My belief is that, as part of the erstwhile Great Central trunk line, the Woodhead route was a victim of pre-grouping and post-grouping rivalries carried into the era of nationalization. Once 'rationalization' became the order of the day, an ex-LNER line that was outwith the sphere of influence of the Eastern or North Eastern Regions was first candidate for elimination. Whilst, in 1960, BR denied rumours that the Great Central main line to London was a candidate for closure, and indeed lip service was paid to the notion of reserving such a route for specialized traffic such as 'Car Sleeper' or 'Starlight' services, no serious thought seems to have been given to 'traffic sectorization by route', if I may coin a phrase. When, some 25 years later, 'sectorization' of BR into six component groups — InterCity, Network SouthEast, Provincial, Freight, Parcels and International — came about, it was, of course, too late to contemplate 'traffic sectorization by route' that might, for example, have seen the Great Central retained as an express freight line, both trans-Pennine and north-south. Obviously it was far too late to prevent the ghastly waste of invested resources represented by the indecently hasty elimination of steam, which itself could have been retained, and eliminated only when time-expired, on selected routes. Yet, as the Great Central was crucified on the altar of 'rationalization', so steam was crucified on the altar of 'modernization'. The same thing happened to trams and the trolley-bus. They are now to be 're-invented'; more of that in a moment. It was amusing — no, pathetic — to note that 'roads lobby' colleagues, bemoaning the loss of the GC route, thought it would have made a good 'coach-way'; but presumably not built, maintained, signalled and policed by the coach-operator!

* * *

From an historic ramble encompassing the era of Medieval mobility, through canals and into the railway age, with a look at what might have been in terms of railway closures, the 'roads and tracks' theme of changing patterns of overland transport can be viewed through the eyes, and in the experience of, those responsible for 'the railway', be they national politicians or individual railwaymen.

One of the problems faced by British Rail as a nationalized industry is its woeful weakness in the face of an all-pervading roads lobby. Well-financed, multi-faceted, often hidden, it has many advocates at West-

minster and amongst manufacturers, operators, users of coaches, cars and commercial vehicles who work alongside road-builders, construction equipment manufacturers and an unseen army of financially motivated men to persuade Government to spend, spend, spend more and more on the roads. Organizations like the AA and RAC abuse their member's fees by purporting to represent 'the motorist' as though he or she never travels by public transport. (I do not want my fees to such bodies to be used for this purpose — all I join for is a breakdown service, not politics, 'cheap' loans or special offers of consumer goods.) Lush directorships or consultancies await those deemed 'useful' by the roads lobby.

Conversely, where or what is the 'rail lobby'? There are the rail unions — but when they can be nullified by 'road' unions like the TGWU. There are rail users — but they have never been mobilized as a campaigning body, and have no 'financial' basis to compare with the structure of the roadmen. There are the past employees, but even to write down this list is to illustrate the inequality of muscular support for a national but state-owned service industry when compared to the money available to rail's main competitors, enjoying the luxury of total taxpayer funding for their 'track'. However, there *is* an army of rail supporters. What they may lack in financial clout is more than compensated for in a wealth of experience, loyalty and dedication — words that would earn a sneer from the Bus & Coach Council or the Road Haulage Association, but which earn respect from any individual citizens.

Having spoken to Lords Marsh and Peyton, I next 'interviewed' two retired railwaymen, one from an earlier generation, who provided me with much education, information and fascination. Gerald Aston and Raymond Fox were introduced to me by a constituent Sid Keeling; they both travelled to London specifically to allow me to 'interview' them. Like most railwaymen — and unlike most politicians — they are wont to keep themselves to themselves. With very few exceptions, most of their experience is in danger of remaining unrecorded for posterity.

Raymond Fox joined the LNER in 1938 as a Clerk. After the war he returned to the LNER, becoming Station Master at Coxwold on the York-Pickering line. After nationalization he was Station Master at New Barnet for five years, then he assumed responsibility, on the Eastern Region, for running the services through what he called the 'traumas of dieselization'. He then transferred to the Western Region, and finally to BR Headquarters on freight operation planning.

Gerald Aston joined the LMS in 1931, spending most of his early years 'in and around Derby'. It would be hard, today, to find a man as fluent with his words, as keen with his memory, yet as extensive in his actual experience of the pre-nationalization railway. Would that I, or someone, had the time and the occasion to extract his memories and put them on paper. His LMS experience rightly earned him an important 'backroom' position in the British Railways world. In 1963,

Opposite *By any standards, the 'Deltic' express passenger diesel locomotives, introduced to replace the LNER 'Pacifics' on the East Coast Main Line, represented a major step in changing the old order. The fact that they lasted a mere 20 years can be attributed either to shorter life expectancy than the steam engines they replaced, or to faster technological change: it depends on your viewpoint. They covered more miles than their steam predecessors in their short lives.*

February 1963 was still bleak, cold and snowy in a vile winter. Late one afternoon I managed to find myself at Welwyn Garden City Station, during the time when Raymond Fox was coping with what he refers to as 'the traumas of dieselization'. The sight of passing 'A3' No 60071 Tranquil and 'V2' No 60906 was reward indeed, and I remember them to this day. As light failed, a 'Deltic' came pounding up the main line, passing the semaphore signals and other paraphernalia of the old order. I did not bother to record the number, recalling only that Gresley's railway would soon be 'out of steam'...

during the Beeching years, he moved to Crewe as Assistant Line Manager; he retired in 1969.

We discussed the state of the railways as they faced mounting competition in the years between the wars, and the early closures of lines at that time. Gerald Aston recalled that the General Strike of 1926 was the precursor, indeed the cause, of some of the early closures, particularly the discontinuance of passenger services. He has particular memories of the Winsford CLC (Cheshire Lines Committee) branch. It is in its way a classic case of the manner in which politics forced a railway company to keep open a line that was patently unprofitable. It is also an early example of 'bustitution', a word of which much remains to be heard. Opened in 1870, passenger services were discontinued between 1872 and 1886, then were reinstated until 1888 when, following an accident, the Board of Trade insisted upon extensive point and signalling improvements. The CLC decided that potential revenue could not justify the expenditure, but the Winsford Local Board appealed to the Railway and Canal Commission, who forced the company to spend the money deemed necessary by the Board of Trade for the safe operating of passenger services. Thus, from 1892 onwards, the CLC was forced to operate an expensive loss-making service. Then, in 1930, the CLC — which had survived the grouping as an independent railway company — issued notices locally of its proposed withdrawal of the passenger service 'twixt Cuddington and Winsford. This time it

was the Winsford Urban District Council that opposed the company and, in effect, sought the re-enforcement of the 1891 Order. The CLC sought to have it rescinded.

As this is not a history of Cheshire branch lines, I must resist the temptation to set out the arguments which finally persuaded the commissioners to find in favour of the Cheshire Lines Committee. The replacement bus service eventually took over the provision of passenger services — but not before a deputation from the local council had finally petitioned the railway company not to hand over the service to the North Western Road Car Company Limited — on the basis that they respond to the despairing plea of the leader of the council, who urged 'For God's sake don't withdraw your trains — there's not enough traffic to pay the working expenses of a daily bus service.'! No more eloquent testimony could be found of the unreasonable expectations already mentioned and nurtured by people about *their* railway.

Gerald Aston remembers the aftermath of the General Strike. 'I think

Opposite *LNER 'C13' 4-4-2T No 67436 stands at Winsford with an RTCS Special in 1953.* (Winsford Local History Society).

Above *Winsford & Over Station in 1910.* (Winsford Local History Society)

Overleaf *Holland Arms Junction, for Pentraeth, Anglesey, 1 July 1908.* (Gwynedd County Libraries)

HOLLAND ARMS
FIRST TRAIN TO PENTRAETH
July 1st 1908

it is fair to say that the first closures were after the General Strike in 1926. Half-a-dozen lines had never reopened after the Strike, mainly passenger. On the LMS, Red Wharf Bay closed in 1931.' Raymond Fox added that, also in 1931, 'all the intermediate stations between York and Seamer Junction, Scarborough, closed, except two.' A number of branch lines were closed in 1930, too.

We next discussed the 'Square Deal' campaign, a subject that might well benefit from detailed scrutiny as discussion about privatization progresses. In essence, Messrs Aston and Fox expressed the view that the camaraderie at all levels, from Chairman to porter, a feature of what we now call 'industrial relations', that existed in the days of the Big Four and before, was lost under nationalization. All staff were exhorted to encourage the travelling public to use the railways: there was a family atmosphere, albeit a very large family. Then came nationalization.

'Personally I hated it,' said Gerald Aston. 'I became District Officer at Derby in 1948. We were confronted with trivialities pushed upon us by Labour people who had been brought in, notably Benstead of the NUR, as Deputy Chairman of BTC, and W.P. Allen, who had been General Secretary of ASLEF, as Staff Supervisor. Their influence very much reached our life. Allen's main object was to take as many privileges from the officers as he could: spite and politics.'

So what, I asked, was morale like amongst those who were actually running the railway?

'In the days of the LMS you knew you were somebody. You knew the directors. The directors came round the country and talked to you.'

Although this familiarity was followed by faceless anonymity, did he feel that in more recent years there had been a better atmosphere?

'I retired in 1969. To some extent there was a better atmosphere, particularly after Brian Robertson left. He was a very austere man, who made no attempt to get to know people.'

So there had been improvements in morale?

'Despite the upheavals of Beeching's time, there was an improvement in morale. He came round to see people, although his assistant, Philip Shirley, was the railwayman's *bête noire*. He came to lunch and started setting about us — none of us were any good. Freddie Simpson, who was one of the local managers, turned on Shirley and said: "If you had been any bloody good, you would have grown square peas so that you could pack more into the tins when you were at Batchelor's". Shirley got up and walked out.'

Of Shirley, Richard Hardy says that he was 'feared by some, disliked by others, respected by quite a few, including the author. On a visit, he would ask one half-a-dozen questions at once. Try to answer all six and one would be sunk without trace.'

We talked of other personalities; Aston added the terse comment: 'People did not trust Marples'. We then turned from people to events and talked about the 1955 Modernisation Plan. Whilst admitting to having no sentimentality for steam, Gerald Aston felt that the attempt to 'dieselize everything' was done too quickly. The steam fleet steadily became neglected and ill-maintained, yet with frequent diesel failures ill-conditioned steam locomotives were expected to operate diesel schedules. I recalled the event in 1987, when steam returned to the Salisbury-Yeovil line.

'Look at *Clan Line*; it was on the Salisbury-Yeovil line and was called on to run a service train after a diesel breakdown. In fact, it knocked two minutes off the time. The condition of the locomotive bore no resemblance to the general condition of the steam fleet in 1962-8. If the engines had been in the same condition as this one, the world would have been a different place. Do you subscribe to the proposition that we should have had a policy of concentrating steam on certain lines and maintaining it properly and utilizing the investment in Standard classes, whilst phasing in diesels more slowly?'

There followed a discussion on the merits of the Riddles '9F' 2-10-0, which all agreed had been an exceptional engine. Gerald Aston com-

Overleaf *Gerald Aston recalls with favour his memories of the '9F' 2-10-0, which he described as an 'exceptional engine'. Indeed it was, and in its destruction is epitomized the waste of resources inherent in the mass scrapping of steam. As a memento of his years at Derby, here is No 92030 on shed there on 9 September 1966, five months before withdrawal.*

In January 1982, Class '27' BRCW Type 2 Bo-Bo (what a mouthful!) No 27012 heads south out of Aberdeen, passing Ferryhill Junction. The city's main passenger station, Aberdeen Joint, was the meeting-place of the Caledonian and Great North of Scotland railways. Ferryhill Junction was the point at which the much-lamented Ballater branch of the GNSR turned inland. Ferryhill Shed was hard by the Junction; once the home base of the last 'A4s' on main-line duty.

Perhaps the most interesting feature of this photograph is not the locomotive, but the gantry in the background. The semaphore arms have just been removed, but the Caledonian ironwork is still in place.

mented that most of the class 'had six to seven years service at most. They came to my notice on the Washford Heath-Carlisle.' We then discussed diagramming and utilization. Aston said: 'Mass utilisation was introduced in 1930. The Preston loco in 1933 did Manchester-Liverpool-Glasgow-Preston. By 1934, with the Stanier "5" they started through working and intensive diagramming spread very extensively. Crewe to Perth, then Aberdeen and back to Crewe. Sixteen out of 24 hours working. E.J.H. Lemon, Vice President of the LMS, introduced intensive diagramming.'

Raymond Fox added: 'I was at Paddington when we had to do the submission for the HST. The CME said he would require 84 per cent usage of the stock. As an operator, I said you cannot do it. Seventy-five per cent should be the maximum. But to make the submission work in the east versus west battle, we wanted to get the best figure.'

We then reverted to the 'investment' aspects of the Modernisation Plan. The concerns amongst the three railwaymen were that the Plan was insufficiently forward-looking. Raymond Fox: 'The Plan was largely based on plans produced by the railways at the end of the war. In 1944 the LNER published a plan which was carried forward into the 1955 Modernisation Plan with very little change. It was insufficiently geared

up for forward planning; there was not enough planning in 1955.' This is an LNER man speaking, and it could be said that the 1955 BR plan was more ambitious than the 1944 LNER proposals — perhaps not surprising 10 years after, rather than one year before, the end of the Second World War.

Gerald Aston, obviously speaking with the conviction of personal memories, expressed in few words the view that negative rather than positive attitudes prevailed. 'The Plan devoted a great deal of thought to what track we could do without for the electrification, so that we didn't wire up more than was necessary, bearing in mind factors like sidings, loops, etc. I don't think it is unfair to say that this atmosphere permeated the railway scene, so that later, arising out of Beeching, there were too many people in high places who were prepared to go along the line "anything you can do, I can do better" in terms of closures and so on. We fought against a number of closures, but were over-ruled, for example on the Leicester to Rugby line which would now be an invaluable connection.'

How did they fight; did they put up figures?

'Yes, fighting against regional general managers. You were just told: "We are going to close it".'

So the costing-out exercise was a charade?

'Just about.'

Sid Keeling, also in the front line at the time, used the destruction

Stanier 'Black Five' 4-6-0s, referred to admiringly by Gerald Aston with reference to intensive diagramming, were introduced by the LMS in 1934, and they lasted literally until the end of steam.

Here, at Bolton MPD on 25 June 1968, No 45104 is at home. The mechanical coaling plant was built by the LMS in 1936. Since then, the only additional facilities to be provided were new lavatories in 1937. The shed, coded 9K in September 1963, survived almost until the end of steam; indeed, in January 1967 over 50 steam locomotives were still allocated here. This is the last week of life of Bolton MPD steam working; indeed, five days after I took this photograph, the shed closed and was soon totally demolished.

Northampton MPD in the days Sid Keeling remembers. Versatile Horwich 'Crab' No 42723 from Agecroft (26B) potters about the shed yard on 7 July 1963. Under the grime hides a black locomotive.

of the Blisworth-Northampton line as an example of an unwise decision. How Sid's words rang in my ears on Monday 20 November 1989. Arriving at Euston to catch the 08.52 to Northampton, due in at 10.07, there began a catalogue of incompetence and aggravation that saw me arrive — eventually — at Northampton at 11.20, by an unintended and unwelcome 'diversion' via Rugby! *If the Blisworth-Northampton line still existed, we could have overcome the problem caused by a derailment 'twixt Roade and Northampton.* How prophetic of Sid, and how apposite an example he gave me, unwittingly.

Raymond Fox, from his Western Region time, bemoaned the singling of the Salisbury-Exeter — don't we all! He said: 'Certainly I had very personal doubts about things like the Exeter-Salisbury line singling. It was forced through. I was at Paddington at the time — LSWR/GWR competition. My experience of single-track working was on the branch line from Pickering to York. You got messages asking why a train was five minutes late. If you did not get a freight through at a particular time, you could delay it by 2-3 hours. But when you are talking about singling a main traffic route, I could not follow the logic. How could a train service be operated in this way? How do you maintain the track?

'I was new to the Western when all this was going on at the end of 1967. We demonstrated from the operating side how impractical it was. Little hiccoughs at either end which would cause delays. Being a new-comer to the Western, I did not have in my mind the geography of the line. I just felt in my bones that it was wrong. My chief was not in favour, but the General Manager in discussions could not justify keeping it!'

Gerald Aston added: 'As far as closures were concerned, I think we

The interregnum 'twixt steam and diesel is captured here at Paddington in January 1963 in a photograph that I had relegated to my 'useless' box due to the prominence of the 'Western' diesel and the unobtrusiveness of the steam engine. Before you say that my initial judgement was correct, note, too, the long-disappeared GWR colour-light signals, once such a distinctive feature of the Paddington scene.

(continued overleaf)

(continued from page 73)

My disinterest resulted in failure to record the number of the 'Western' bringing her train into the Arrivals side, or the class of steam engine, probably a '15xx' large pannier tank hauling empty stock into the Departures side.

In the distance, what is probably a 'Castle' on a Hereford and Worcester train, approaches the end of its journey. These services saw the last main-line steam-hauled workings to and from Paddington.

The 'Western' class 2,700 hp Co-Co diesels are now, amongst a certain fraternity, fondly remembered, and seven of the class, the last of which was withdrawn by BR in 1977, have survived into preservation. Built to replace the GWR 'King' Class 4-6-0s, it is hard for me to raise any enthusiasm for what is, and will always be, merely a mechanical box, to be switched on and off.

went too far. Not so much the closing of individual stations, but the fact that there was no east-to-west line south of Peterborough/Leicester. This was a great mistake. Oxford-Bletchley should not have been cut out. As far as the Great Central goes, I had to implement this when I was at Derby.'

The final part of this — to me — fascinating triologue concerned privatization. Bear in mind that the participants included a Conservative Party Branch Chairman, and one who described himself as 'right of centre'. Let Gerald Aston have the last word: 'Very dubious. Despite everything, we have got a national system operating, which you didn't in the days of the companies. Birmingham is the hub of it; York is the second hub. We are already suffering from sectorization.

4
THE VERWOOD
SYNDROME

The so-called 'Beeching report' is, as has already been pointed out and contrary to popular belief, not an enormous tome, reaching conclusions based on detailed and cool analysis of all the social, political, economic and prescient factors. It contains just 60 pages of text. Reading it today one cannot help, frankly, but be struck by its superficiality, although that is the fault not of Beeching, but of his political masters. However, as Lord Marsh stated, the fundamental conclusions reached by Beeching were based on one very serious, but fundamental, error: namely that any given line could be categorized as a 'sheep' or a 'goat' by 'analysing' it, as a separate entity, as 'profitable' or otherwise.

The broad conclusions were, however, inescapable — 41 per cent of the system (branch lines and secondary cross-country routes) accounted for only 1 per cent of receipts — but the detailed analysis left a lot to be desired. In 1962, traffic costing was a recognized skill, but without the help of computers or allocation of resources to sectors, was a blunt instrument with which to calculate the costs and revenues of individual route sections.

Traffic costing attempted to allocate costs and receipts to individual flows of freight traffic on specific branch lines or main line services. It was based on an analysis of locomotive and rolling-stock diagrams, paybill costs at stations and depots and even fuel and stores where these could be identified. In 1962, however, many assets were 'common user' — used by several services. Locomotives may have worked a mix of freight and passenger services, depots provided locomotives for several routes, and staff might handle stopping and express passenger, freight and parcels traffic, all in the course of a single shift.

Typically, it might be possible to achieve an accurate allocation of only a third of the actual costs to any one traffic flow or line. The remaining two-thirds would be 'allocated' costs. The cost of junction stations, depots, workshops, district offices, advertising and claims might all be allocated in this way. This was reasonable to give a rough indication of the overall balance sheet, but was quite inadequate in terms of showing:

West of Ringwood the River Avon forms the boundary 'twixt Dorset and Hampshire. By January 1989 the bridges across the river and its adjacent spur formed an increasingly precarious footpath between Avon Castle and Ringwood: still a 'transport link', but a blatant, visible snub to those who regret the destruction of the original east-west railway line hereabouts, known locally as 'Castleman's Corkscrew', after the Wimborne solicitor who masterminded the Southampton to Dorchester railway, of which this was originally part.

a) The avoidable costs, such as redundancy payments and continuing structural maintainance, etc, if a service were withdrawn or a line closed.

b) The potential for cost reduction by substituting diesel multiple units for steam trains, introducing pay train operations or simplified signalling, for example, as pioneered by Gerard Fiennes in East Anglia.

c) The potential for revenue generation by service restructuring or changes in local fares or freight rates.

Most importantly, no attempt was made to measure value for money of the services provided, other than that of profit or loss to the Board, using the inadequate techniques described above. Modern commercial methods of using market research to determine acceptable fare-levels on different services had not yet appeared on the scene. The socioeconomic effects were considered only briefly in a dismissive way at the end of the report. Only in the case of commuter services around

London and other major provincial cities was it conceded that the railway had an important role in the continuity of the business life of the city in restricting traffic congestion and spreading development benefits over a wider area and that this might justify financial support. In London, the conclusion was that substantial real pricing, coupled with reducing peak resources, would eventually bring commuter services into profit.

Significantly, no measure of social value is possible, as passenger miles are not quoted in the table of examples given as 'typical passenger services'. Nevertheless, from the figures quoted it is clear that there was a wide variation in support levels for different services, with surprisingly cheap costs in Scotland and rather heavy costs in the West of England.

In examining the effect of Beeching in South East Dorset/South West Hampshire, for example, we can note that lines were closed that could today fulfil a vital role, whilst those that survived have seen services expanded and, in the case of Southampton-Portsmouth, electrification being sanctioned on a line that is duplicated by the M27 motorway, itself opened long after Beeching. The lines that were closed cross an area that has seen a population explosion. The accompanying map illustrates what happened.

The area covered by the map actually encompasses parts of Dorset,

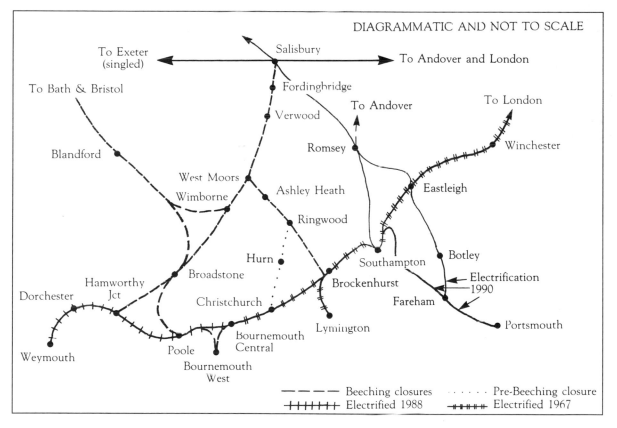

DIAGRAMMATIC AND NOT TO SCALE

To Exeter (singled) · Salisbury · To Andover and London

To Bath & Bristol · Fordingbridge · To Andover · To London

Verwood

Blandford · Romsey · Winchester

West Moors · Ashley Heath · Eastleigh

Wimborne

Ringwood

Hurn · Southampton · Botley

Hamworthy Jct · Broadstone · Brockenhurst · Electrification 1990

Dorchester · Christchurch · Fareham

Weymouth · Poole · Bournemouth Central · Lymington · Portsmouth

Bournemouth West

— — — — Beeching closures · · · · · Pre-Beeching closure
+++++++ Electrified 1988 · +++++ Electrified 1967

Above and above right *Both West Moors and Verwood lost their railway stations and railway lines at the moment of the explosion of motor car ownership in the mid-1960s. How my constituents now wish that they could go quickly and easily by train to the centre of Poole/ Salisbury/Bournemouth, rather than struggle in by bus or by car and search for a car parking space. A road has now cut a swathe through the site of the signal box. (Memory Lane Picture Company, Parkstone).*

Hampshire and Wiltshire. As Regional Government does not exist, and as each county has its own Structure Plan, those with, at the very least, no interest in the railway have well and truly had their way. Let us look at Dorset.

That Verwood has just translated itself from a village to a town is an item of news that has not impinged upon the columns of the national newspapers; likewise, the change of nomenclature of the Wimborne Council into 'East Dorset'. Yet change and growth in population are — or should be — one of the most potent forces in determining the style and extent of public transport provision. Whilst the Beeching proposals for railway development, and for railway curtailment, were scrutinized and debated in the '60s, one wonders how much simultaneous attention was paid to patterns of population change.

As far as I am aware, Britain does not have a 'population policy', either in terms of individual family planning or in terms of overall national strategy. For the former we should be grateful; for the latter we should be ashamed. The Department of Employment accumulates statistics in what are euphemistically called 'travel-to-work' areas; yet who in Government pays attention to emerging patterns by which people do actually travel to work? By what possible logic do we assume that, in growth areas, roads must be built from funding out of taxation, whilst new railway lines, or new stations on existing lines, must be funded by British Rail from their operating revenues? Thus I decided to try to investigate the reasons for such omissions, and to do so by using — some might say abusing — my parliamentary position to try to obtain answers to such questions.

Verwood itself today, but barely recognizable by most of my constituents who live in what was a village and now calls itself a town, albeit without the consent of many who live there. With a population in excess of 10,000, it is a classic example of developer-led growth. Neither a market town, a manufacturing centre, a river confluence or a cultural centre, Verwood was successfully targeted by profit-driven housebuilders. Its railway is but one piece of absent infrastructure, which once saw the Salisbury to Bournemouth line cross the bridge, photographed in December 1988.

As I write these words, there has just ended the Examination in Public (EIP) of the Dorset County Council's proposed changes to their existing Structure Plan. The overriding item is the 'demand' for ever more homes. This demand emanates from those with a commercial or professional interest in population growth, be they landowners, housebuilders, developers, architects, ambitious local authority officers or empire-building councillors, lawyers, accountants — almost everyone except the *people* who live in the area. Naturally, there is some discussion about roads, mainly the need for upgrading, widening, or simply *more*. Of railways there is scant mention.

The detectable pattern is that the Thatcher decade has resulted in assumptions of increasing reliance on meeting *popular* needs — for homes, cars, personal mobility — whilst bringing about decreasing reliance upon planned and integrated public transport. This, perhaps, is a generalized, even facile, comment. It takes no account of the large-scale investment in the railway system elsewhere that has taken place in the '80s, albeit mainly on the Intercity railway where profits are realizable. Network South-East, too, has managed significantly to reduce its call on the taxpayer, at the bidding of Government; but whether this has been achieved by sacrificing safety, punctuality, cleanliness or comfort is a matter of intense political debate. But claims that 'British Rail made a profit in the financial year just ended' (1987-8), used as a pretext by political apparatchiks to push the case for privatization, actually weaken that case when the figures are scrutinized. That 'profit' relates to the sale of land. On some of that land, trains once ran. If transport patterns change, as they have at Verwood, the value of that 'profit' will be negative, not positive, to the community.

In a letter to me dated 28 March 1988, the then recently appointed Dorset County Surveyor, David Hutchinson, reports on my request for information about 'the present or planned transport use of old railway formations'. Bear in mind that, by this date, the population explosion in the area was well and truly a reality. He states the County Council's Structure Plan policy as follows: 'When considering the future use of redundant railway routes, first priority will be given to their use for transport purposes.'

Before, however, you assume that 'transport purposes' might naturally include reinstatement of railway services, his factual report to me provides the following details:

Length of railway	Present/proposed use
West Moors-Ashley (near Ringwood)	'Trailway' opened 1987
Roman Road Creekmoor-Merley	'Trailway' opened 1986

Stark reminder of yesteryear, the telegraph pole stands silent vigil on the trackbed of 'Castleman's Corkscrew' beside the bridge athwart the Avon's spur, to the west of Ringwood. The line closed on 16 October 1966, having been opened by the LSWR in 1847. Between this bridge and Ringwood Station lay the junction of the original line to Christchurch, opened in 1862. When what became the main — and is now the only — line through Christchurch was opened, in 1888 via New Milton, the line illustrated here became a secondary route; whilst the Ringwood-Christchurch (via Hurn) line became a mere twig. It was closed as long ago as 30 September 1935.

Where that railway used to run: and how we wish that it did, still. Wimborne and Blandford have changed, as rural life is overwhelmed by urban-orientated activity and mobility. This is the S & D bridge over the River Stour at Sturminster Newton. The erstwhile small towns at the heart of the countryside pierced originally by the Dorset Central and Somerset Central railways, feel the pincer of pressure at both ends, as Bath and Bristol, Poole and Bournemouth, seek to extend their influence, road pressure and congestion grow, and we are left only to mourn the shortsighted selling-off of land that once provided a transport link.

Merley-Lake Gates — Part used by A31 Wimborne Bypass opened 1981

Broadstone-Fleetsbridge — Broadstone Link Road and cycleway under construction

Branksome Triangle, East — A338 Branksome Relief Road, forecast completion 1993

Spetisbury-Charlton Marshall — Formation purchased by County Council for possible use as A350 bypass. Scheme not programmed

Shillingstone — Formation purchased by County Council for possible use as A357 bypass. Scheme not programmed

Refer to my map on page 77 and look at what has happened on the section of line 'twixt Poole and Ringwood, passing through Broadstone,

Wimborne, West Moors and Ashley Heath, all areas where the population has increased explosively since the line closed. The Poole to Ringwood Railway was first mentioned in a report on Public Transport following the publication of the county's Land Use and Transportation Study in 1967. It envisaged that some form of rapid transit system could serve the substantial residential areas close to the line both existing and proposed.

Subsequently, the Draft Poole District Plan published in 1973 included a policy which precluded development from taking place on the railway line which would prejudice the establishment of a rapid transport system serving Creekmoor, Broadstone and Merley. The Broadstone Central Local Plan was approved by Poole Borough Council in 1976 and states the need to avoid prejudicing a rapid transport system with an interchange and associated car park on railway land in the Plan area.

At the Planning Sub Committee on 2 June 1978, a Report by the

Other cross-country routes that succumbed just as motor car ownership exploded, and which served towns at each end with burgeoning populations, were the Horsham-Guildford and the Horsham-Brighton lines. Both lines served what were once scattered rural communities, but are now in commuterland, towns where car-parking is, for many, a nightmare.

In their declining years, both lines were operated by Ivatt LMS taper-boilered Class '2' 2-6-2T locomotives. Here, on 2 January 1965 — the last day *(continued overleaf)*

(continued from page 83)
of steam-operated services on the Reading-Guildford-Redhill-Tonbridge line — No 41301, with 75A Brighton shedplate and an 'SC' indicating a self-cleaning smokebox, runs light-engine through Guildford station en route to the shed. She had in fact disgraced herself that day, with dropped fire-bars resulting in her replacement by sister engine No 41294 on the resultant much delayed 13.34 Guildford-Horsham train.

How can anyone compare such a sight, with another locomotive in the distance, with today's utterly featureless motive power?

County Planning Officer into the future use of the disused railway land between Poole and Wimborne was considered and it was resolved that in view of the appraisal carried out as part of the South East Dorset Structure Plan, the reservation of this land for a long-term alternative transportation system was not justified.

The Structure Plan for South East Dorset was subsequently approved by the Secretary of State for the Environment in February 1980. It makes no reference to a rapid transit route.

The Chairman of the County Council's Planning & Transportation Committee is one of the leaders of the 'development faction' in Dorset. Her attitude to the railway is well illustrated by her successful opposition to BR obtaining the contract to carry BP oil by rail from Wytch Farm. Between Government 'policy' for the use of, or disposal by, BR of 'surplus land', BR itself, in following Government policy, and vandalism, as exemplified by Dorset County Council, any chance of reinstating rail services in this overcrowded, congested and overdeveloped piece of England, have totally and inexorably vanished for ever.

One of the main problems of railway development all over Britain was the inherent assumption, dating from the dawn of the railway age, that 'all routes lead to London'. Any student of development in the industrialized world can see that precisely the opposite has occurred, as capital cities have become overcrowded. Whether one looks at the United States, West Germany, Canada, France, it is the growth of the provincial cities that has taken place. Avoiding London is the priority for millions of people; yet look how we have either destroyed or failed to make the most of our cross-country routes. Birmingham-Southampton is an obvious example. Whilst nationalization has overcome the GWR/LMS competition by developing Coventry-Leamington-Banbury, part of this route is single track; further south, the lessons learned during the war of the value of lines like the Didcot, Newbury & Southampton did not save it from closure and destruction. Why must we *destroy*, even it we deem it necessary to discontinue services? Try travelling from Oxford to Northampton today by rail, or, say, Redditch to Coventry.

The Docklands Light Railway illustrates what *can* be done when lines close, but infrastructure remains. As David Mitchell, then Minister of State for Public Transport, admitted to me in a letter dated 13 January 1988, '. . . it was recognized that light rail would provide the sort of flexibility which would enable the existing disused rail infrastructure in Docklands to be exploited by linking them together'. In pursuing the facts surrounding the DLR's construction, I was told by Keith Bright, former Chairman of London Regional Transport, in a letter to me dated 8 June 1988: 'We estimate that approximately two-thirds of the DLR was constructed on former BR property. It is difficult to say with precision what the additional cost would have been had this land and structures not been available, but the total capital cost might have been of the order of half as much again as the actual cost of £77 million.'

As I write, it seems that Bournemouth, like Southampton and many

other cities, is now beginning to plan for what is euphemistically called a 'People Mover'. Described as a 'safe, pollution-free and fast method of transportation that eases the traffic burden on congested roads' (*Bournemouth Evening Echo*, October 1988), it sounds to me remarkably like an electric railway...

Such thoughts prompt me to wonder why we so rarely ever marry old-fashioned convenience to modern technology. Slip coaches enabled passengers to enjoy fast trains not otherwise available. Electric or even diesel power provides the facility for 'powered slip coach' operation which surely merits examination. Yet my attempts to persuade BR to examine the idea are met with faint amusement and no interest. Perhaps it is nonsense, but perhaps, just perhaps, it is an idea worth contemplation.

Ridicule was the reaction to another suggestion I made, some years

Banbury today is served by inter-regional trains utilizing former LMS and GWR tracks to provide an important and growing through service; it has lost its other cross-country links, especially to the Great Central, so vital in times of emergency. In the late evening of 9 September 1966, '8F' 2-8-0 No 48669, with 'sans serif' plate but shedplate gone, stands stoically under the gaze of the driver. Note the turntable in the background.

Surviving into the 'eighties, this splendid gantry at the west end of Southampton station epitomizes the 'railway furniture' that lent character, colour and individuality to the railway scene. At the time of its replacement by the ubiquitous colour-lights, it was claimed to be the largest remaining semaphore gantry on BR.

before it became fashionable. The *Financial Times* in August 1972 reports my questions to the then Minister for Transport Industries, Mr John Peyton. Asking him 'what studies his Department had made of the contribution which could be made by trams in solving urban transport problems', the Minister told me that his officials 'would look carefully at continental urban transport systems, including tramways which had been used by cities that had modernized their transport systems.'

The purpose of this passing reference to trams is twofold: to give a nod in the direction of tracked transport, noting that this abandoned and derided form of transport — in Britain's cities if not elsewhere in

Europe — is making a comeback; and to recall that the rise of the tram was a factor in the decline of many of our suburban railway systems.

Finally, to sum up this saga of lost opportunities, I cannot resist, in relation to the line from Poole to Ringwood, including an extract from an article in *The Railway Magazine*, Volume LV, dated 1924. This extract covers the comments about West Moors, in my constituency, the population of which, since 1924, has grown from 750 to 7,150.

'Passing Holes Bridge level crossing, the railway enters the county of Dorset about a mile to the east of West Moors station. At West Moors the old main line is at its nearest point to Bournemouth, the distance being approximately 5 miles from the boundary at Moordown, to which point the Bournemouth tramway system at present extends. West Moors is the junction station for the Salisbury line, and in consequence has the advantage of two good routes to London, namely, that *via* Brockenhurst, where the Bournemouth expresses are joined, and also *via* Salisbury, joining the

South from Verwood lies West Moors, like Verwood also preyed upon by developers. Here, one line turned north towards Verwood — its track ran between the trees beyond the tarpaulin hut. To the right of the picture ran the line through Ashley Heath and Ringwood, both of which have grown out of all recognition since the demise of the railway. As is evident, total obliteration of West Moors junction is but days away. In the line's time it provided a through route for excursion trains — Cardiff to Bournemouth, for example — to avoid congestion and reversal at Southampton.

Whilst Verwood has grown from a village at the behest of developers, the inexorable growth of major cities like Bristol has seen small market towns like Thornbury converted to commuterland dormitory suburbs. The erstwhile Midland Railway's branch from Yate — itself similarly developed and now with its closed railway station re-opened — encapsulates the lost opportunities for the railways created by political short-sightedness. The Thornbury branch was closed, then reopened as far as the quarry at Tytherington, but never reopened to prosperous Thornbury because of its severance by — yes! — a motorway. Here, Yate Junction, to the north of that re-opened station, leaves those who know the area and who believe in 'the railway' enraged at opportunity lost.

West of England expresses. The local train service to and from Bournemouth, Wimborne and Weymouth is also much more frequent than at Ringwood and Holmsley, owing to the addition of the Salisbury trains, which stop at West Moors to and from Bournemouth.

The village itself is a growing one and is fast becoming a suburb of Bournemouth. A few years ago there was scarcely a house in the place, but during the past decade new roads, shops, and residential buildings have been erected in every direction. The higher portions of the village on the south-eastern side have been strongly recommended by medical men to invalids requiring a bracing and invigorating atmosphere, and it is on these open spaces on the Bournemouth side of the railway that the village must eventually grow. The uninterrupted view of several miles from this point is very beautiful, especially in the early summer and autumn when the heather is in full bloom on the open moors, with the background of the fine verdure of the New Forest in the distance.

Among the growing industries of West Moors is a pig and poultry farm recently established on co-operative lines by ex-Service men. Here they have provided their own sausage and cooked meat factory, with an increasing output each year as the venture becomes known. A very fair traffic from this source is dealt with at West Moors station. In addition there is a large traffic in trees, shrubs, fruit, flowers, &c. The village is supplied with the Bournemouth water and gas, and is in direct telephone communication. In competition with the railway, a frequent service of motor buses runs to and from Bournemouth. The residents are principally of the retired tradesmen and professional classes. Most of the residences are surrounded with pleasant gardens and lawns. They have a recreation hall, a church and a Congregational chapel; and at Ferndown, within easy distance, are fine golf links, while the village forms a good centre for many trips by rail and coach. There are boundless walks over the open moorlands and pine woods, where one can roam at will. The staff at West Moors station consists of a stationmaster, Mr Wright (at one time chief clerk at Bournemouth Central) and five men. Not only is the station traffic increasing yearly, but there is also a very fair transfer traffic *via* Salisbury to South Wales, the West of England, London and the Midland Counties.'

This, then, concludes the 'Verwood Syndrome', the use of a specific example to illustrate a general problem. The dictionary describes 'syndrome' as 'any combination of signs and symptoms that are indicative of a particular disease or disorder'. That seems to me adequately and fully to describe the syndrome of wasting known transport assets, particularly related to railways. Let us hope we *see* the cure; we do not need to look very far, for it is indeed staring us in the face. The reference, above, to competing bus services in dated 1924. By how much has road congestion hereabouts increased? To ask the question, and to lament the destruction of the rail option, is answer enough.

In the next chapter, I concentrate on the current comparisons in the relationship between HMG and BR on the one hand, and the French Government and SNCF on the other. The rules relating to line closures, service discontinuance, track disposal and so forth could not be more different. Under existing French law, what happened in Dorset simply could not happen.

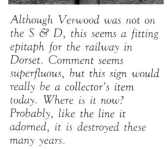

Although Verwood was not on the S & D, this seems a fitting epitaph for the railway in Dorset. Comment seems superfluous, but this sign would really be a collector's item today. Where is it now? Probably, like the line it adorned, it is destroyed these many years.

5
FRENCH CONNECTION

Opposite *What, you might ask, is the point or purpose of including a photograph of Redhill shed in a chapter entitled 'French Connection'? Because it is on this land, now derelict but still in BR ownership, that I am advocating the construction of a rail flyover to carry the SECR Tonbridge-Redhill-Reading line over the Brighton lines. That SECR line was built with the Channel Tunnel in mind: its upgrading and incorporation within the Tunnel rail link plans seems to me, and increasingly to others, to be an obvious and an essential 'London avoiding line' for rail traffic, especially freight, seeking access to and from the North and West of Britain, for Tunnel-bound traffic.*

Thus, for 'French Connection' via Redhill, let this photograph continue to remind those who resist my proposals outlined in Tunnel Vision *of the SECR line's potential for the future.*

Maunsell SR 'S15' 4-6-0 No 30847 blows off on shed on 16 April 1963.

Glance at the advertisements in the railway magazines, and you will be assailed with blandishments to visit exotic locations in the Far East, or South America, to record the final months or years of steam operation on their railway systems. To those prepared to accept unquestioningly the company of unselected fellow enthusiasts on expensive expeditions to countries whose railway history is unremarkable, such advertisements doubtless appeal, and I can well understand if not share such an appeal. Yet the environment of 'the railway' itself provides just as strong — or almost as strong — an appeal. Mechanical hardware is not the only attraction. If it were, then a non-steam railway would be totally devoid of any interest, and a journey by bus would be as interesting as a rail journey. For me this will never to be true; nor, I suspect, will it be so for legions of railway enthusiasts.

In this post-Beeching era, around Britain there survive, sometimes precariously, the remains of countless destroyed railway lines, as varied as the great swathe of the Waverley Route 'twixt Carlisle and Edinburgh or an insignificant little single-track branch such as that to Shipston-on-Stour in Warwickshire to take at random two bits of the jigsaw, or spider's web, that once made up the railway map of Britain. Surely I am not alone in seeking such remains as may exist of any line when time permits of exploration when in the vicinity of a closed and lifted track?

We bemoan the destruction of our great railway heritage. The same short-sightedness and municipal vandalism that destroyed our urban tramways has been writ large by railway management and politicians this last half century and more, as the transport arteries created by the blood, sweat, toil, tears and cost of building up our railway system, have been quite deliberately closed down, sold off, ploughed up, built over and eradicated from the landscape. Thus the pleasure and interest in 'the railway' is now reduced for most enthusiasts either to a study of the archaeology of the industrial revolution in Britain, or to a visit to a narrow gauge line on a sugar plantation in the Philippines to see a steam engine at work. As Poland, Turkey, East Germany *et al* complete the elimination of steam, intercontinental travel becomes the only means of satisfying our eternal search; or does it?

On our doorstep — indeed quite literally thus by 1993 — stands a country with a better appreciation of the value of the work of our fore-bears in the field of railway construction. Where we have destroyed, they have retained much of their all-embracing rail network. Where we have forced freight on to the roads, they have continued to provide industry and commerce throughout the country, at hundreds of towns, villages and remote communities, with a rail option. In France, the rail-way is an appreciated, recognized and integral part of the national trans-port network. Whilst France leads the world in its appreciation of the use of the railway in the 21st century, it also pays its respect to its his-tory by retaining countless miles of track that would have succumbed to the Beeching Axe. On many of these lines, buildings and railway archaeology survive, to the joy of those who go to look. For most Brit-ish enthusiasts, the sole point of contact with French railway history revolves around the name Chapelon, who perhaps was to French steam in its latter years as was Churchward to the railways of Britain. But if your interest in railway history extends beyond the smokebox — read on.

In looking at the differences in *attitude* to railways in Britain and France, and relating them to custom, practice and, indeed, legislation, I hope to show why and how these differences exist; thereafter we can have a brief look at a few illustrations of where they exist.

Opposite *Colour photographs of French steam at work seem rare. Here, at Nice MPD in May 1964, is SNCF '141R' 2-8-2 No 1156. The TGV is not yet a gleam in a Frenchman's eye.*

If the enthusiasts' market in France could match its British counterpart, it would be possible for me to record No 1156's home shed at this date; its previous and future allocation; its date and place of withdrawal; and its ultimate destination and fate. I know none of these things. What is known, however, is that 1,340 American and Canadian built 141Rs were hurriedly constructed and delivered after the war in order to overcome the French motive power shortage.

Of typically American design, the '141R' was fuel-hungry. French modification included the smoke-deflectors. The similar French-designed version of what, in effect, became to France what the 'Black Five' was to BR, was the '141P', once described in relation to the '141R' as 'akin to that between a Ford and a Rolls-Royce'. Of the last thousand steam locomotives at work in France at the end of the 1960s, more than two-thirds were 141Rs.

Try as I might, I have failed to find any English-language books dealing in any depth with the French attitude to their railways. Thanks, however, to assistance from Christian Masset, First Secretary at the French Embassy in London, my attention was drawn to their Internal Transport Act of 1982. This stemmed from experience gained from previous attempts to define the relationship and establish the framework within which three partners should work together: Central Government for funding, Regional Government for transport planning, and SNCF for operating the railway.

Following on from this Act there came a 'Planning Contract', signed in April 1985 between SNCF and the State. Protestations from my Parliamentary colleagues, the Ministers in the Department of Transport, about my preference for methods employed or policies pursued by our neighbours, came in two varieties: either 'the French Government's criteria for investment by SNCF are the same as we apply to BR'; or, when pressed for details, they say 'we don't understand the French Government's rail investment criteria'. The former statement is inaccurate, the latter convenient. In relation to what is happening in Britain, the French are light-years ahead of us, in attitude, in determination, but above all in sheer scale of financial commitment.

It is tempting to detail, at length, the contents of the 'Planning Contract'. I had been made aware of its existence during a visit to the Department of Transport in Paris in September 1988. The purpose of my visit was twofold: to investigate the apparent mystery of French railway investment policy, and to enquire as to why so many little-used branch and cross-country lines survived in France.

The answer to both questions can be found in the single word 'politics'. In a nutshell, it is political will that sustains a high level of investment, via the taxpayer, in French railway modernization; and it is political pressure, both from the trade unions and local political interests, that keeps so many rural lines open.

Contrary to the protestations of successive Secretaries of State for Transport since the election of Margaret Thatcher's first Government in 1979 — Norman Fowler, David Howell, Tom King, Nicholas Ridley, John Moore, Paul Channon, Cecil Parkinson — there *is* a difference between the railway investment policies pursued in Paris and those pursued in London. In my discussions with the French Department of Transport, the *only* perceived similarity between the criteria sought by the French Government from SNCF, and the criteria sought by HMG, was in the rate of return, namely 8 per cent in both Britain and France. But — and it is a huge but — the factors which SNCF can include in their projections are fundamentally more comprehensive than those available to BR. They include:

Environmental considerations
Social factors
Protection against noise
Land use

Landscape
Minimal use of agricultural land
Reduction in time lost through congestion
Indirect benefits, eg planning projects
Regional policy

The mere act of writing these down causes me flushes of anger at the
narrow and restrictive pressures applied by the Treasury towards public investment in our railways.

   In order to ensure that my information on this subject was accurate
I asked M Claude Gressier, Directeur des Transports Terrestres, if he
would provide for me a document setting out in full the information
I sought on French policy, both in theory and in practice. Thus, in
due course, there arrived on my desk a *magnum opus* of information.
Thanks to Christian Masset, this valuable document had been expertly
translated into English: together with my notes, I am reasonably con-
fident that the information is accurate! Amongst the additional infor-

mation are the full details of the Planning Contract between SNCF and the State, signed in April 1985 and covering the years 1985-89.

The whole document is peppered with phrases which would give a British Treasury Minister a heart attack. The most obvious cause of misery to those in charge of our purse-strings is the simple paragraph: 'The French government is financing 30 per cent of the infrastructure costs. The SNCF is having recourse to borrowing on the capital market for the remaining 70 per cent.'

You need to be neither a mathematician nor a magician thus to define the fundamental financial differences in the climates facing SNCF and BR. Whilst 70 per cent of SNCF's investment financing will be secured through direct borrowing on the French and international markets, 100 per cent of BR's investment comes from its own sources only after approval by HMG; and only for those projects which meet targets that, to SNCF, would appear to be an obstacle race rather than a gate of opportunity. In Britain, the Ryrie Rules established by the Treasury rigidly curtailed private sector investment, just to ensure that BR faced the greatest hurdle. The Ryrie Rules were 'retired' in May 1989. They were formulated in 1981 by a National Economic Development Council Working Party under the chairmanship of Sir William Ryrie, then Second Permanent Secretary to the Treasury. The original intention of the Ryrie Rules was to establish criteria under which private finance

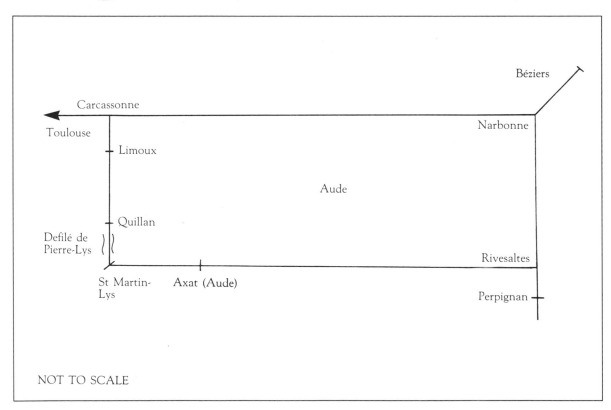

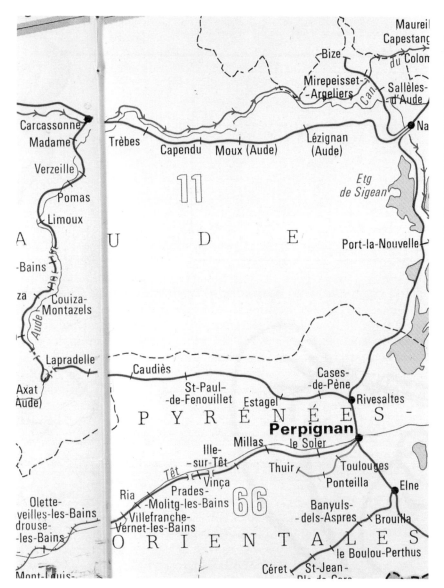

Left and overleaf *Contrary to appearances from the SNCF map (left), travel from Carcassonne to Perpignan via Quillan ('missing' from the map but the next station north of Axat) by rail is no longer possible (see page 110). Passenger services by dmu, as shown on the SNCF timetable overleaf, run only between Carcassonne and Quillan. The freight service from Rivesaltes westwards runs only to a point just beyond Axat (see page 113).* (Map courtesy of SNCF)

could be introduced into the nationalized industries. The Rules were revised in February 1988 to take account of the privatization of many previously nationalized industries and the introduction of new forms of private sector involvement in public services through contracting-out, opting-out, mixed funding and partnership schemes. However, with the recent announcement in the Government White Paper of increased public funding for roads, many contractors questioned why they should take the increased risks and up-front costs associated with private sector projects, when they could achieve proven levels of return and plenty of guaranteed work from planned Government projects.

There it is in a nutshell. The taxpayer pays for the roads, so why

433   RAPPEL : Ⓐ Tous les jours sauf samedis, dimanches et fêtes   Ⓑ Tous les jours sauf samedis   Ⓒ Samedis, dimanches et fêtes

Carcassonne ■━━━━━━━━━━━✗━━━━━━━━━━━■ Quillan

			8281	8283	8287	8291	8293	8295	987
		Identification	8281	8283	8287	8291	8293	8295	987
		Qualité	AUTORAIL	AUTORAIL	AUTORAIL	AUTORAIL	AUTORAIL	AUTORAIL	AUTOCAR
		Places assises	1-2	1-2	1-2	1-2	1-2	1-2	2
		Particularités					⌖	⌖	
		Circulation	✗						10
Tab	Km	Origine	■	■	■	■	■	■	■
	0 **Carcassonne**		6 34	8 19	12 15	14 57	17 14	18 24	20 20
	9 Couffoulens-Leuc ⊙ SB		6 43	✗ 8 28	12 24	✗ 15 05	✗ 17 22	18 34	✗ 20 30
	12 Verzeille		6 48	8 35	12 29	15 10	17 27	18 39	✗ 20 35
	16 Pomas ⊙ SB		6 52	✗ 8 39	12 33	✗ 15 14	✗ 17 31	18 44	✗ 20 43
	26 Limoux		7 03	8 49	12 43	15 24	17 41	18 57	20 55
	35 Alet-les-Bains ⚠		7 11	8 57	12 51	15 33	17 50	19 05	✗ 21 10
	42 Couiza-Montazels ⚠		7 19	9 05	12 59	15 40	17 58	19 13	21 18
	45 Esperaza		7 23	9 09	13 03	15 44	18 02	19 17	✗ 21 22
	48 Campagne ⊙ SB		7 27	9 13	13 07	✗ 15 48	18 06	19 21	✗ 21 26
	54 **Quillan** A		7 34	9 20	13 14	15 55	18 13	19 28	21 35
	Terminus		■	■	■	■	■	■	■

10 • les Ⓢ sauf les 25 XII , 1er I et 13 V ;
• les 10 XI , 24 , 31 XII et 11 V .

Opposite *Train Number 8293, the 17.14 from Carcassonne, has just arrived at Quillan on 22 September 1987. Arrival time is timetabled for 18.13 — notice the station clock. The trailer unit is conveyed on the morning and evening trains to and from Carcassonne respectively, and will be stabled at Quillan whilst the power car makes a further round trip before the day's end.*

This is the view northwards, towards Limoux and, 54 km distant, Carcassonne. At present, rail freight services run throughout between Carcassonne and Quillan. Rumours exist that freight services may terminate at Limoux, with 'fercam' beyond. 'Fercam' is the description of road haulage under railway management, 'fer' being an abbreviation of 'chemin de fer', (continued on page 97)

should private sector investors bother to finance them? However, no such luck for BR — *they* must fund all their own construction, and account for it annually. In France, 'the State makes a financial contribution to investment deemed to be in the national interest', in accordance with the commitments made in Article 27 of the Planning Contract. The assistance given to SNCF is calculated in such a way as to prevent the schemes concerned adversely affecting their finances. Set at 30 per cent of the infrastructure cost (excluding interest during construction) of, for example, TGV Atlantic, State assistance has been fixed at one-third for the electrification designed to end the isolation of Brittany and the Massif Central.

I am writing this at the time when BR is unable to meet the Government's investment criteria to electrify the line from Redhill to Reading, let alone even to contemplate the project I submitted in *Tunnel Vision — Rail Routes to the Channel Tunnel* (Conservative Political Centre, July 1988) of electrifying the existing line between Folkestone-Redhill-Reading-Oxford-Banbury-Coventry with 25kv, to enable the Midlands, Merseyside, North-West and Scotland to take full and proper advantage of the Channel Tunnel. Frankly, it makes a mockery of Ministerial protestations that the distant regions of Britain should benefit from the Tunnel.

How much more need I quote from the Planning Contract? Amongst the criteria employed in assessing the case for investment is included 'social benefits'. The success of the TGV Paris-South East (TGV-PSE), completed to Lyon in 1983, is already evident beyond peradventure but in Britain it would never have been built. Solely used by special electric multiple units travelling at an end-to-end maximum speed of 270 km per hour (167 mph), the project's rate of return is now 15 per cent. It moved into financial surplus after covering all financial and operating charges in 1984. The loans should all be repaid before the end of 1992. The current (1989) position is as follows:

'Between 1980 and 1987, on the lines currently served by TGV-PSE, the volume of the SNCF's main line passenger traffic rose by about 70 per cent; the increase was almost exclusively due to TGV-PSE; without it, the volume of that traffic would have remained stagnant since 1980.

'Between 1979 and 1986, on the lines currently served by TGV-PSE, the volume of first-class passenger traffic greatly increased; over the same period, on the sections of the SNCF's South-East network today not served by TGV-PSE, the volume of that traffic markedly declined.

'In 1987, more than 16.5 million passengers travelled 9.9 billion passenger-km by TGV. Growth is continuing steadily and

(continued from page 96) and 'cam' an abbreviation of 'camion' (lorry). As my SNCF collaborator indicates 'you are not likely to find these terms in the Petit Larousse (not yet anyway)'. He usefully further informs me that 'from this root, other words have sprung — fercamisation, fercamier — (je fercamise, nous fercamisons)'.

Note the bull-head rail in the foreground, and the 'informal' arrangements for crossing the track at this remote point on SNCF's passenger network.

Opposite *With the 1,288m Picoulet de Quirhaut in the background, a single unit diesel railcar departs from Quillan, emitting diesel smoke, with train No 8294, the 18.27 to Carcassonne, on 22 September 1987. Also visible is the red and cream trailer car seen in the previous picture. It will remain here until the 6.32 departure the following morning.*

This view southwards towards Axat is somewhat misleading, as the tracks have been severed and through working southwards and eastwards to Axat, Rivesaltes and Perpignan, from Quillan, is no longer possible. Nevertheless, Quillan station, open for freight and passenger traffic, remains active, albeit not the double-ended railhead it once was.

From Axat, 11 km south of Quillan, the freight service to Rivesaltes is secure, there being steady traffic from the quarries along the line. As quarry lorries pound the country lanes in Somerset, Dorset and Wiltshire, we can only envy French rail freight policy.

the first months' results for 1988 show a 4 per cent rise in the number of passengers on all routes and of almost 7 per cent on the Paris-Lyon-Saint-Etienne-Grenoble line.

'Between Paris and Lyon, TGV-PSE's entry into service has led to a loss of about 50 per cent for the commercial airline, Air Inter, while on its other internal French routes, that company recorded an increase of 80 to 100 per cent between 1980 and 1986.

'Finally, because the new high-speed line is used solely by long-haul passenger trains and the more or less parallel conventional line by regional and local passenger and freight trains, the route's freight capacity has increased and freight trains' average operational speeds and punctuality have both improved.

'The commercial successes achieved were a deciding factor in the French Government's decision of 9 October 1987 to build a bypass round Lyon and a first stage of TGV-PSE's extension towards the Mediterranean coast, to Valence.

'This new line, about 116km long, will diverge from the existing high-speed Paris-South-East line at P.K.380 (Montanay), north of Lyon. It will run through four departments, Rhône, Ain, Isère and Drôme. It will serve Satolas airport, to the east of Lyon. It will intersect with the existing Lyon-Chambéry-Grenoble line. The bypass will rejoin the existing Valence-Grenoble line at Saint-Marcel-lès-Valence, north-east of Valence.

'The bypass will be engineered for 300 km/h and should cut the journey time between Paris and Valence to 2 hours 20 minutes (at an end-to-end average speed of 220 km/h) and that between Paris and Marseille to 4 hours 10 minutes.'

The second major project, TGV Atlantic (TGV-A) is now under construction. Again, the French Government is financing 30 per cent of the infrastructure costs. A partial service opened (Paris-Le Mans) in September 1989, and the south-western branch (Paris-Tours) 'will come into service in summer 1990. The complete high-speed service — it goes even faster, 300 km/h, or 186 mph — with all its extensions, will be inaugurated in October 1991.' No 'ifs'; no 'buts'.

The TGV North (TGV-N) project was investigated back in 1974, at the time of the abortive Channel Tunnel project abandoned by the incoming Labour Government. (However much I may criticize the rail investment policy of the present Government, they are fulsome indeed when compared to the actions — if not the words — of erstwhile Labour Governments; but that is another story.) TGV-N was aborted, but was reinstated following the decision of the French, Belgian and West German Governments to initiate the study of a fast Paris-Brussels-Cologne (PBK) link. 'Regional planning considerations led to the decision to serve the metropolis of Lille, occupying a favourable position in the geographical area served by the projects connected with TGV North.'

When comparing the situation pertaining in Britain and France

respectively, do not forget that all these French lines are *new* railways. Here, the electrification of the East Coast Main Line — 150 years old — is considered to be a monumental investment decision. If one was writing a 'British TGV' scenario, just imagine its contents. Nothing better illustrates the paucity of our efforts than the following notes concerning the interconnection of TGV networks to the east of Paris:

'The idea behind TGV Interconnection is to weld together all TGV routes. The same trains may be used for cross-country passengers and those starting or ending their journeys in Ile de France, with a view to increasing train frequencies, cutting travelling time

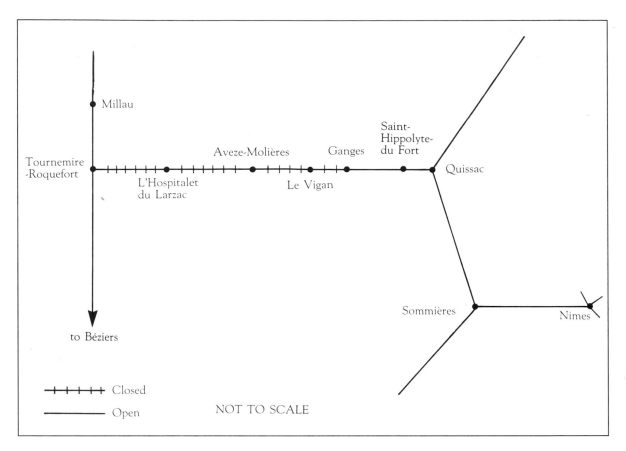

Above and right *Le Vigan was once the centre-point at which lines met eastwards from Tournemire-Roquefort and westwards from Quissac. A small, isolated town reached across rugged terrain, it is surprising that, until very recently, it retained any rail connection (see page 114).* (Map courtesy of SNCF)

and reducing time spent changing stations in Paris.

'This relieves the Paris main line termini of unnecessary transit traffic and delays the advent of their saturation point. On the South-East route, the project also relieves the Paris-Lieusaint section, which is already very congested, particularly at Villeneuve-St-Georges.

'Furthermore, the TGV fleet's overall profitability has improved thanks to the creation of direct Paris-service ("Passe-Paris") trains, avoiding the unproductive turn-round time in termini currently without any turn-round facilities.

'This project ends the traditional structure of the French rail network inherited from the nineteenth century, in which most cross-country passengers had to change trains and stations in Paris. Substantially improving the opportunities for unbroken journeys between the various French provinces, this project is of great importance for French regional planning.

'About 104km of new track is to be built.

'The interconnection will make a junction with TGV North, cross land covered by Paris-Charles de Gaulle airport, where an underground station is planned, and run south to the Coubert interconnection triangle, where one arm will head for the Grande Ceinture orbital line round Paris and the conventional Paris-Lyon line, with a junction in the vicinity of Valenton, and another will connect with the new TGV South-East line at Moisenay. The interconnection with TGV Atlantic will be made by means of the Grande Ceinture Orbital line between Valenton and Massy.

'This project's infrastructure cost is estimated at around 5.4 billion francs (1985 values), including the new TGV stations of Roissy-Charles de Gaulle and Melun-Sénart. An additional investment of 860 MF (1985 values) for rolling stock will be necessary to operate this infrastructure.'

'The rate of internal return on the investment will be around 10 per cent.

'The SNCF will finance the project through loans and, for the stations, through contributions from local authorities and other bodies that will benefit from the building of TGV North.'

The fifth TGV line, TGV East, connecting SNCF with the railways of Switzerland, Germany and Luxembourg, is projecting a rate of return

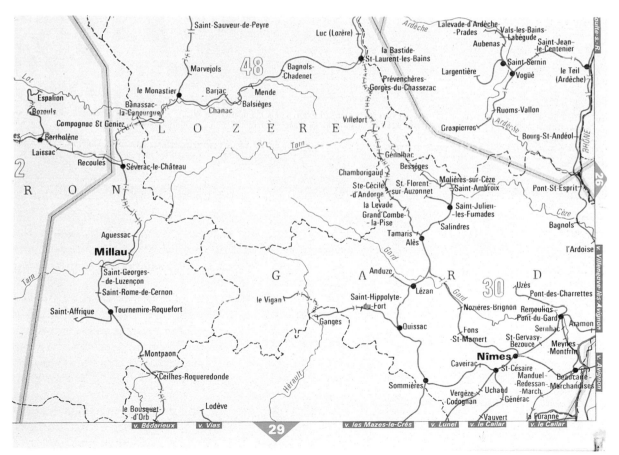

Precise information as to the closure of the line westwards from Le Vigan to Tournemire has eluded me: my SNCF informant says that it was 'ages ago'. Certainly by September 1981 the track through the western part of Le Vigan had been lifted. Hopefully the stonework and metalwork will survive as a memento, or an 'urban walk', although the town is small, agreeable and largely unspoiled.

on investment 'of the order of 4 per cent'; unthinkable in Britain, but acceptable in France, where this attitude towards railway development is infecting the continent. The Channel Tunnel will enable us to join in, but at present we seem to prefer congestion, pollution and playing politics with our railways. I find it all very sad and frustrating.

As if all this development of the 'new' railway was not enough, legislative changes governing the relationship between SNCF, Central Government and provincial authorities have brought about a dramatic improvement in SNCF's local services. For more than ten years this sector has seen consistent growth. The 1982 Internal Transport Act enabled regional authorities to sign agreements with SNCF which permit them to assume the role of the Government without losing the Government's financial contribution. As a result, more regional authorities are developing regional provincial services in co-operation with SNCF. The contrast is an important force in regional planning poli-

413 | RAPPEL Ⓐ Tous les jours sauf samedis, dimanches et fêtes Ⓑ Tous les jours sauf samedis Ⓒ Samedis, dimanches et fêtes | **413**

Bagnères-de-Bigorre

Tarbes ■━━━■ La Mongie

Km	Origine	784	784	764	766	786	786	822	770
	Identification	784	784	764	766	786	786	822	770
	Qualité	AUTOCAR	AUTOCAR	AUTOCAR	AUTOCAR	AUTOCAR	AUTOCAR	AUTOCAR	AUTOCAR
	Places assises	2	2	2	2	2	2	2	2
	Particularités								
	Circulation	[10]	[11]	[12]	[13]	[14]	[15]	✕	[16]
	Origine	■	■	■	■	■	■		■
0	**Tarbes**	(7.00	(7.00	8 15	(9.05	(10.40	(10.40	(12.05	(12.05
2	Seméac-Marcadieu ⊙	x 7.07	x 7.07		x 9.13	x 10.47	x 10.47	x 12.12	x 12.13
5	Soues ⊙	x 7.14	x 7.14		x 9.18	x 10.53	x 10.53		x 12.18
7	Salles-Adour ⊙	x 7.16	x 7.16		x 9.21	x 10.56	x 10.56		x 12.21
9	Bernac-Debat ⊙ SB	x 7.19	x 7.19		x 9.24	x 10.59	x 10.59		x 12.24
10	Bernac-Dessus-Arcizac ⊙ SB	x 7.22	x 7.22		x 9.26	x 11.01	x 11.01		x 12.26
12	Vieille-Adour ⊙ SB	x 7.24	x 7.24		x 9.28	x 11.03	x 11.03		x 12.28
13	Hiis ⊙ SB	x 7.26	x 7.26		x 9.30	x 11.05	x 11.05		x 12.30
14	Montgaillard ⊙	x 7.28	x 7.28		x 9.31	x 11.07	x 11.07		x 12.31
16	Antist ⊙ SB	x 7.29	x 7.29		x 9.33	x 11.09	x 11.09		x 12.33
17	Ordizan ⊙ SB	x 7.30	x 7.30		x 9.35	x 11.10	x 11.10		x 12.35
19	Pouzac ⊙ SB	x 7.35	x 7.35		x 9.40	x 11.15	x 11.15		x 12.40
22	**Bagnères-de-Bigorre** A	(7.40	(7.40	8 50	(9.45	(11.20	(11.20		(12.45
	Bagnères-de-Bigorre	■	7 45	8 55		■	11 25		■
25	Aste (Pont de) ⊙ SB		7 58	9 08			11 38		
28	Campan ⊙ SB		8 06	9 16			11 46		
33	Ste-Marie-de-Campan ⊙ SB		8 25	9 35			12 02		
41	Artigues ⊙ SB								
47	**La Mongie** A		8 45	9 55			12 20		
	Terminus	■		■			■	Tournay	

Km	Origine	824	772	774	832	834	776	778	780
	Identification	824	772	774	832	834	776	778	780
	Qualité	AUTOCAR	AUTOCAR	AUTOCAR	AUTOCAR	AUTOCAR	AUTOCAR	AUTOCAR	AUTOCAR
	Places assises	2	2	2	2	2	2	2	2
	Particularités								
	Circulation	[17]	✕	[18]					
0	**Tarbes**	(12 15	(14 35	(16 00	16 10	17 10	17 10	19 05	21 00
2	Seméac-Marcadieu ⊙	x 12 22	x 14 42	x 16 08	x 16 15	x 17 15	x 17 19	x 19 13	x 21 07
5	Soues ⊙		x 14 48	x 16 13			x 17 24	x 19 17	x 21 11
7	Salles-Adour ⊙		x 14 51	x 16 16			x 17 26	x 19 18	x 21 13
9	Bernac-Debat ⊙ SB		x 14 54	x 16 19			x 17 29	x 19 20	x 21 16
10	Bernac-Dessus-Arcizac ⊙ SB		x 14 56	x 16 21			x 17 31	x 19 22	x 21 18
12	Vieille-Adour ⊙ SB		x 14 58	x 16 23			x 17 33	x 19 24	x 21 20
13	Hiis ⊙ SB		x 15 00	x 16 25			x 17 34	x 19 25	x 21 22
14	Montgaillard ⊙		x 15 02	x 16 26			x 17 36	x 19 26	x 21 24
16	Antist ⊙ SB		x 15 03	x 16 28			x 17 38	x 19 29	
17	Ordizan ⊙ SB		x 15 05	x 16 30			x 17 40	x 19 30	
19	Pouzac ⊙ SB		x 15 10	x 16 35			x 17 45	x 19 35	
22	**Bagnères-de-Bigorre** A		(15 15	(16 40			17 50	19 40	21 35
	Bagnères-de-Bigorre			■		■			■
25	Aste (Pont de) ⊙ SB								
28	Campan ⊙ SB								
33	Ste-Marie-de-Campan ① SR								
41	Artigues ⊙ SB								
47	**La Mongie** A								
	Terminus	Lannemezan			Montréjeau	◆			

[10] ● ✕ et sauf le 13 II
[11] ● le 13 II
[12] ● du 19 XII au 17 IV tous les jours
[13] ● jusqu'au 18 XII et à partir du 18 IV tous les jours
[14] ● du 4 I au 3 II et du 29 II au 25 III les ①, ②, ③. ④ et ⑤

[15] ● du 19 XII au 3 I : tous les jours;
● du 9 au 31 I les ⑥ et ⑦.
● du 4 au 28 II tous les jours.
● du 5 au 27 III les ⑥ et ⑦.
● du 28 III au 17 IV tous les jours
[16] ● les ④ sauf le 12 V :

● le 11 V
[17] ● les ⑥ sauf les 7 XI, 26 XII, 2 I, 20, 27 II, 2, 9 et 16 IV
[18] ● du 19 XII au 3 I les ⑤, ⑥ et ⑦.
● du 9 I au 17 IV les ⑥ et †

cies, in which rail plays an important — and accepted — part: Dorset County Council please note.

All these thoughts were brought to mind by my meetings in Paris. Before turning to look at the branch and cross-country lines, with their SNCF bus services, my mind drifted off to recollections of steam at Monte Carlo, and the roundhouse at Nice engine shed. On a memorable visit to the area, *en route* to the Monte Carlo rally in May 1964, we found ourselves arrested and taken to the Police Station in a small town near Vichy. Perhaps a word of explanation is necessary.

In company with Arthur Carrington and two others, whose names sadly now escape me, we set off in a single-engined Meta-Sokol — a Czechoslovakian crop-spraying machine as I recall — to fly to Nice. We left Gatwick, at the time little more than a rough strip, 17 per cent over our maximum permitted weight. We were promised a following wind. The met report was wrong; we were running out of fuel; we landed

Above and overleaf *'That the branch line to small towns like Bagnères-de-Bigorre, Sarrancolin, Louchon or Saint-Girons survive is remarkable' (page 115). The maintenance of rail freight services, and the inclusion of SNCF autocar routes within the timetables above and overleaf, provides accessible information both for locals and more distant travellers. Well-used goods yards attest to the success of the SNCF 'marchandise' policy and to the environmental advantages of keeping (some) heavy lorries away from the centre of small towns.*

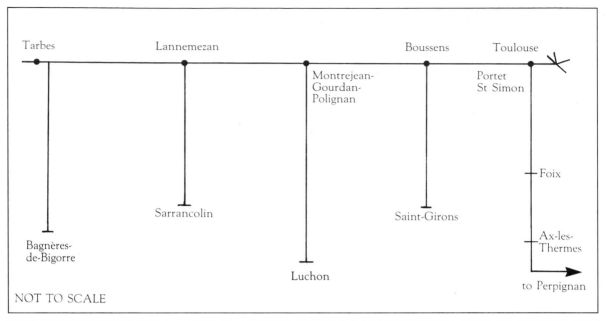

Tarbes — Lannemezan — Boussens — Toulouse
Montrejean-Gourdan-Polignan
Portet St Simon
Sarrancolin
Saint-Girons
Foix
Bagnères-de-Bigorre
Luchon
Ax-les-Thermes
to Perpignan

NOT TO SCALE

---

438   RAPPEL Ⓐ Tous les jours sauf samedis, dimanches et fêtes   Ⓑ Tous les jours sauf samedis   Ⓒ Samedis, dimanches et fêtes   **438**

St-Girons

Boussens ■■■■ ━━━━━━━━━━━━━━━ ■ Guzet-Neige

Identification	221	223	223	225	225	227	229	231	245	233	235		239		243
Qualité	AUTOCAR	AUTOCAR	AUTOCAR	AUTOCAR	AUTOCAR	AUTOCAR	AUTOCAR	AUTOCAR	AUTOCAR	AUTOCAR	AUTOCAR		AUTOCAR		AUTOCAR
Places assises	2	2	2	2	2	2	2	2	2	2	2		2		2
Particularités															
Circulation	✗	🔟	⑪	⑫	⑬	✗		Ⓒ	⑭	Ⓐ	✝				⑮

Tab Km	Origine	221	223	223	225	225	227	229	231	245	233	235		239		243
0 **Boussens**		(7 11	(8 22	(8 22	(10 47	(10 47	(13 06	14 40	(16 01	(17 50	(18 54	(19 45		20 07		(22 06
2 Roquefort-sur-Garonne ⊙ SB		x 7 15	x 8 24	x 8 24	x 10 50	x 10 50	x 13 09	14 43	x 16 04	x 17 53	x 18 56	x 19 48		x 20 10		x 22 09
6 Mazères-sur-le-Salat ⊙		x 7 18	x 8 28	x 8 28	x 10 54	x 10 54	x 13 11	14 47	x 16 08	x 17 57	x 19 00	x 19 52		x 20 13		x 22 12
10 Salies-du-Salat ⊙		(7 20	(8 30	(8 30	(10 58	(10 58	(13 14	14 51	(16 12	(18 01	(19 04	(19 56		20 17		(22 16
12 Mane ⊙		x 7 24	x 8 34	x 8 34	x 11 03	x 11 03	x 13 19	14 56	x 16 16	x 18 06	x 19 08	x 20 01		x 20 22		x 22 21
13 Touille ⊙ SB		x 7 25	x 8 37	x 8 37	x 11 04	x 11 04	x 13 20	14 57	x 16 17	x 18 07	x 19 09	x 20 02		x 20 23		x 22 22
13 His ⊙		x 7 27	x 8 39	x 8 39	x 11 06	x 11 06	x 13 22	14 59	x 16 19	x 18 09	x 19 11	x 20 04		x 20 25		x 22 24
16 Castagnède-du-Salat ⊙		x 7 29	x 8 41	x 8 41	x 11 08	x 11 08	x 13 24	15 01	x 16 21	x 18 11	x 19 13	x 20 06		x 20 27		x 22 26
17 Saleich ⊙ SB		x 7 30	x 8 42	x 8 42	x 11 09	x 11 09	x 13 25	15 02	x 16 22	x 18 12	x 19 14	x 20 07		x 20 28		x 22 27
18 Lacave ⊙		x 7 31	x 8 43	x 8 43	x 11 10	x 11 10	x 13 27	15 03	x 16 23	x 18 13	x 19 15	x 20 08		x 20 30		x 22 29
19 Mauvezin-de-Prat ⊙ SB		x 7 32	x 8 44	x 8 44	x 11 11	x 11 11	x 13 28	15 04	x 16 24	x 18 14	x 19 16	x 20 09		x 20 31		x 22 30
21 Prat ⊙		x 7 34	x 8 46	x 8 46	x 11 13	x 11 13	x 13 30	15 06	x 16 26	x 18 16	x 19 18	x 20 11		x 20 33		x 22 32
26 Caumont ⊙		x 7 40	x 8 52	x 8 52	x 11 19	x 11 19	x 13 35	15 12	x 16 32	x 18 22	x 19 24	x 20 17		x 20 38		x 22 37
27 Sentaraille ⊙		x 7 42	x 8 54	x 8 54	x 11 21	x 11 21	x 13 37	15 14	x 16 34	x 18 24	x 19 26	x 20 19		x 20 40		x 22 39
29 Lorp ⊙ SB		x 7 44	x 8 56	x 8 56	x 11 23	x 11 23	x 13 38	15 16	x 16 36	x 18 26	x 19 28	x 20 21		x 20 41		x 22 40
31 St-Lizier ⊙		x 7 46	x 8 58	x 8 58	x 11 25	x 11 25	x 13 40	15 18	x 16 38	x 18 28	x 19 30	x 20 22		x 20 43		(22 42
33 **St-Girons** A		(7 53	(9 05	(9 05	(11 32	(11 32	13 44	15 25	(16 45	(18 35	(19 37	(20 30		20 47		(22 46
St-Girons				9 05		11 32										
36 Eycheil ⊙				9 09		11 39										
40 Lacourt ⊙				9 13		11 43										
48 Soueix ⊙				9 24		11 54										
52 Seix ⊙				9 29		11 59										
54 Oust ⊙				9 32		12 02										
54 Ercé ⊙				9 44		12 14										
61 Aulus-les-Bains ⊙				(9 55		(12 25										
76 Latrape ⊙				(10 10		(12 40										
82 Guzet-Roc-Blanc ⊙				(10 30		(13 00										
84 **Guzet-Neige** A				(10 35		(13 05										
Terminus				■		■										

🔟 ● jusqu'au 18 XII : tous les jours;
● du 4 I au 2 II et du 29 II au 25 III : les ①, ②, ④ et ⑤.
● à partir du 26 III : tous les jours.

⑪ ● du 19 XII au 3 I : tous les jours;
● du 6 I au 23 III : les ⑤, ⑥, ⑦ et les 4, 5, 8, 9, 11, 12, 15, 16, 18, 19, 22, 23, 25 et 26 II.

⑫ ● jusqu'au 18 XII : tous les jours;
● du 4 I au 3 II et du 29 II au 25 III : les ①, ②, ③, ④ et ⑤.
● à partir du 18 IV : tous les jours.

⑬ ● du 19 XII au 3 I : tous les jours;
● du 9 au 31 I : les ⑥ et ⑦;
● du 4 au 28 II : tous les jours;
● du 5 au 27 III : les ⑥ et ⑦;
● du 28 III au 17 IV : tous les jours.

⑭ ● les ⑤ sauf les 25 XII, 1er I et 13 V;
● les 24, 31 XII et 11 V.

⑮ ● les ⑤, ✝ sauf les 3 IV, 13 et 22 V.

at a French military airfield; it was a few days after the Great Train Robbery, when Biggs and his fellow criminals attacked a railwayman who subsequently died; on landing we were held in custody and thus finished up at the local Police Station. By the time we had convinced the gendarmerie of our innocence, we had lost five hours. We set off for Nice, but with inadequate navigation equipment to fly over the Alps in the dark, settled for a diversion to Marseille where we spent the night.

The following morning we left Marseille at the crack of dawn for the hop to Nice, and on to Monte Carlo by car. Whilst the others watched motor cars race around the streets, I returned to Nice and spent the day with the '141 Rs' at Nice Shed. Writing this down more than 25 years later reminds me also of the sight of steam at Monte Carlo station, incongruous indeed at the Mecca of the smart and fashionable. Seeing again those photographs of steam on the Côte d'Azur a quarter of a century ago provides a suitable entrée to an examination of how French politics is responsible for the survival of much of the French railway system. Thus with this chapter in mind, albeit embryonic, I set out to explore some of the remote and little-used lines that somehow have survived into the last decade of the twentieth century. Is there not a certain irony about a country that simultaneously develops the first 'new' railway in the world, whilst maintaining a service on lines that would have succumbed prior to, let alone after, the Beeching era in Britain?

My ambition to visit Halwill Junction, in North-west Devon, has just been fulfilled. 'Railway politics' in Britain doomed to extinction the former Southern Railway lines west of Exeter. Excepting what is now a suburban branch from Plymouth, and the line to Barnstaple, the lines of the erstwhile LSWR in Devon and Cornwall have gone, save only for the line to Meldon Quarry west of Okehampton, which is still served by engineers' trains for ballast. They were victims of twin forces of destruction. One force was the rivalry 'twixt GWR and LSWR that ensured the demise of the latter's routes just as soon as BR's Western Region took over responsibility for them in the 1960s. The other force was the Beeching Axe. Thus the twin pincers of railway politics and national politics doomed Tavistock, Okehampton, Ilfracombe, Launceston, Bude, Wadebridge, Padstow *et al* to life without the railway; and endless traffic jams, congestion, pollution, frustration and anguish have followed as night follows day. These were the thoughts that crowded in to depress me that day at Halwill Junction, as I recalled my exploration of the extremities of the French railway system in September 1987.

French politics ensured no Docteur Beeching, and their regional policy assures the continuance, as this book is published, of both passenger and freight service, against the odds, on a line that would have undoubtedly succumbed to the Beeching Axe had it been in Britain. It is the line from Carcassonne to Quillan, in Aude Departement.

Overleaf *Searching for something else, I came across this photograph taken during a flying visit to Monte Carlo in May 1964: the rest of the party seemed not to be interested in the last days of the 141R 2-8-2s, one of which stands at the head of a train for Menton. Photographs like this were discarded by me as they reduced the locomotive to a minor role.*

Could one imagine a more poignant and evocative scene? 'Vive la Voiture' would seem to be the epitaph for the railway, or at least for steam. Perhaps it is the incongruity of the backdrop of the shimmering Mediterranean, rather than that of industrial grime, that makes the locomotive seem like an intruder.

Looking north towards Boussens along the lengthy platform at Saint-Girons station, at the end of which I awaited, at Jane's behest, the train that did not come . . .

SNCF diesel engine number Y2482 is stabled alongside the goods shed. Note the goods trucks in the yard on the left of the picture, and the obviously regularly used state of the rails alongside the main platform face. Note also the regional designation, '4', on the buffer-beam of the engine.

Quillan is a small market town about which one could eulogize if writing a tourist brochure. The regional food is exceptionally good, and in September, before the snow brings winter visitors, it is almost devoid of British, or indeed of any, tourists. Enjoying a glass of wine outside a cafe in the market square is, in such circumstances, a pleasure becoming harder to match in these days of mass mobility. I digress.

Quillan itself, in railway terms, is almost at the most distant point of a rectangle, the other three points being the cities of Carcassonne, Narbonne and Perpignan (see the maps on pages 94-5).

The flavour of Quillan can be tasted almost as soon as one leaves, by road, the Autoroute at Perpignan. Modern motorways have a depressing similarity throughout the industrialized world as one approaches the vicinity of a major town or city. From the A9 on to the D117 is, however, a quantum leap. Almost instantly the pace of life changes. Before Quillan the road becomes hemmed in between the infant River

Aude and the craggy outcrops of rock through the Defilé de Pierre-Lys, which account for mineral activity hereabouts. Around Axat, exploitation of dolomite — the double carbonate of lime and magnesium — determines the colour and shape of the landscape. Shades of china clay country — the prevalence of white dust — heighten the kinship with Cornwall. The road dodges into and out of short rock tunnels. To my total unfamiliarity with the railway landscape here was added mystery by the sight of tracks still in use alongside the road from Rivesaltes; then clear evidence of a truncated and uprooted railway beyond Axat. The urge to discover more led us — my long-suffering wife, Jane, trading 'trains-time' for the best dinner in town — to the station.

Quillan Station was very much 'in use'. Questions at the tourist kiosk combined with further attempts with my schoolboy French at the station itself, enabled me to obtain the rough idea. Further 'research' via

Looking north from the Hautes-Pyrénées terminus of Bagneres-de-Bigorre in September 1987. A delightful small town on the River Adour at the foot of the mountains, Bagnères seems to have avoided being over-run by heavy lorries through the maintenance of its rail freight service which, as can be seen, brings plenty of freight traffic to the town.

As elsewhere, the SNCF station is impressive, immaculate and in use, not only for freight traffic but also for the SNCF bus service to (continued overleaf)

(continued from page 109)
*Tarbes. Once a day there is a
'non-stop' in each direction,
with full details incorporated
into the SNCF timetable. In
this way there is — dare I use
the word — an integrated road
and rail service. There is a
handful of buses also from
Bagnères-de-Bigorre up to the
ski resort of La Mongie, albeit
virtually deserted out of season.*

*The freight service on the line
is a possible candidate for
'fercamisation' (see pages 96-7),
but this may not occur due to
the existence of the 'Soulé'
railway-coach factory on the
line.*

the SNCF timetable, questions to the freight service manager, and some
exploration at track level were augmented, on returning home, by reference to Volume 3 of a splendid series of books titled *Trains Oubliés*,
by José Banando.

The key to comprehension of the pattern of service to Quillan is determined by two factors. Firstly, no through rail service between Carcassonne and Perpignan via Quillan is, or ever was, contemplatable, for
there is a main line round the north and east sides of the rectangle
(see the map). Thus, journey times between these cities are around 90
minutes. Quillan, therefore, has always been, for passenger services,
the terminating point of trains from Carcassonne and from Rivesaltes.
Secondly, as far as 'co-ordinated' freight service on both 'sections' of
line is concerned, such through working as existed was eventually terminated by a landslide in 1951 at Pierre-Lys, cutting the roads and temporarily isolating Axat. Yet, even this landslip, which initially affected
the road but eventually the rail service, too, and which of course
accounts for the now disused track between Axat and Quillan, was
not the beginning of a story that makes the line of considerable interest
to anyone who is a student of railway matters.

Immediately prior to the PO-Midi merger, Dietrich railcars were
introduced in 1937 northwards from Quillan, replaced by Renault vehicles in June 1939. Prior to this, electrification had been considered.
However, the Quillan-Rivesaltes service remained steam operated. Then,
in the spring of 1939, what in today's language would be called 'busti-

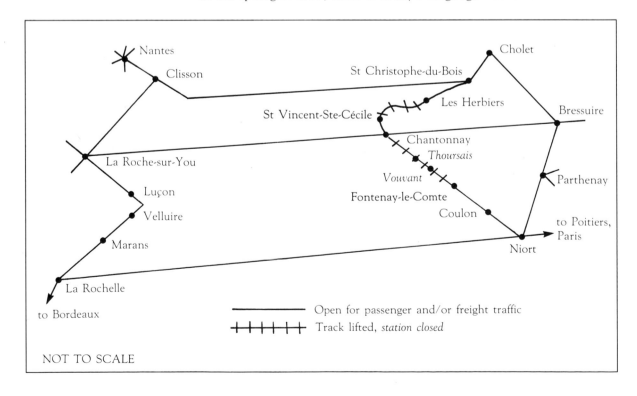

NOT TO SCALE

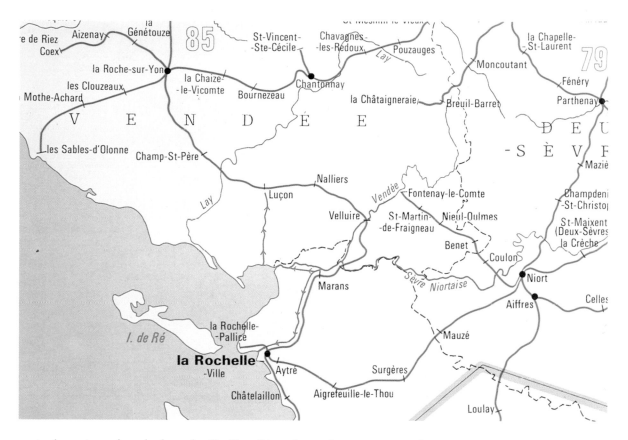

tution' was introduced when the Quillan-Rivesaltes rail service was withdrawn, and the same treatment was meted out to the Quillan-Carcassonne service the following year. Luckily — or, as it is France and not Britain, luck had little to do with it, as the French do not vandalize their railways even when services are withdrawn — when the road service proved unsatisfactory a daily rail service was reintroduced between Carcassonne and Quillan. In June 1943, an odd experiment, which proved successful, involved the conversion of a carriage into a natural gas 'tender' fuelling a railcar. This service, with four trains daily, continued until 1946. Then SNCF put forward yet another proposal to end the Quillan-Carcassonne rail service and replace it with a bus service. Public outcry in Aude prevailed. The rail service was reprieved. It survives to this day, as can be seen from the photographs on pages 97 and 99. What, on Ordnance Survey maps here, would have appeared as 'Tk of old Rly', still shows up on Michelin map No 86 as the railway line.

On the Quillan-Rivesaltes section, history has played its part in the line's fortunes. The landslip at Pierre-Lys in 1951, resulted, for a few days, in the extension of the Carcassonne-Quillan railcar service to Axat as a shuttle service. (In Quillan I was told that services on the section of line between Quillan and Axat had been abandoned in 1943.) By

Left and above *The SNCF map above locates Marans, Fontenay-le-Comte and Coulon, photographs of which appear in the next few pages. The sketch map, left, covers a larger area. See page 118 for details of the lines referred to, but no longer connecting the small towns and villages. (Map courtesy of SNCF)*

This semaphore signal is obviously still in use on the secondary main line at Marans, between La Rochelle, La Roche-sur-Yon and Nantes. Note also the hand-lever for points, and the vintage telegraph poles. In the background is a substantial crossing-keeper's cottage.

this time, the last of the 4-6-0s from Perpignan shed had been withdrawn as motive power for the daily Rivesaltes-Quillan freight, and had been replaced by American-built diesel locomotives based at Béziers, in what José Banando describes as 'one of the great experiments in diesel traction made by SNCF'.

From my observations, the railway line from Rivesaltes appears now to terminate near St Martin-Lys, at the eastern end of the Defilé de Pierre-Lys, although the current SNCF atlas of freight lines still shows the line running through to Quillan, which visibly it does not. How, and if, and when, precisely, the landslip that cut road access between Quillan and Axat back in 1951 related to the discontinuance of services on that section of railway track in 1943, as mentioned, is beyond my comprehension of the French language, and it is marginal to the story, albeit fun to investigate! The point to make — yet again — is that changing circumstances have changed traffic patterns, and thanks to French Government policy of not perfunctorily permitting the ploughing up of railway lines, the Rivesaltes-Axat line has seen increasing freight traffic. The recommencement of the quarrying of dolomite at St Martin-Lys; more dolomite plus chalk fertilizers at Axat; feldspar and timber at Lapradelle; and cement and marble at Omaya, have all contributed to the resurgence of this arm of the 'Quillan Rectangle'. In 1987, there was still a daily freight service on the line, although the

For SNCF, the timetabled Autocar services are professionally operated by a vehicle clearly identifiable with the national railway system, as is evident here with the departure from Fontenay-le-Comte station.

Above *Station detail: could it be* malva trifida, *or yet a puny* ficus?

passenger service had long gone.

Here, then, is the personification of the difference in attitudes and in financial regimes pertaining in France with SNCF as opposed to Britain and BR. With six daily passenger trains, plus one SNCF bus service, in each direction between Quillan and Carcassonne, and the healthy freight service between Axat and Rivesaltes, it would be a pleasant, if forlorn, hope to find a British transport Minister visiting the area.

Less fortunate than Quillan is Le Vigan. Once upon a time it was the centre point on a long cross-country route across the Cevennes from Tournemire-Roquefort, south of Millau, to Quissac, *en route* to Nimes, although the history of the line is dictated and written — as indeed it was operated — as two quite distinct railways. The western line, from Le Vigan to Tournemire, was part of the Midi system, whilst eastwards from Le Vigan, it was part of the PLM system (see the maps on pages 100-1).

In contradistinction to my diagram, the line from Tournemire-Roquefort to Le Vigan, at the heart of the Cevennes, crosses mountainous terrain through a barren region with a harsh climate. Con-

struction, which began in 1885, took 11 years. At L'Hospitalet the line reached the highest point on the land mass between the waters of the Atlantic and the Mediterranean at the Vassal Pass, crossed at an altitude of 808 metres. It was a line of tunnels, viaducts and cuttings, many visible from the D99 which road often shares the route with the railway. It is, incidentally, a part of France still mercifully free of the ravages of mass tourism. Banando's description of the line, translated for me by Jean-Pierre Loubinoux of SNCF as 'irregular', sounds much more attractive in French as 'ce parcours particulierèment tourmenté. . .'. In 1924, the journey time for the distance of 62km 'twixt Le Vigan and Tournemire-Roquefort was around 2½ hours.

As with Quillan in the 1930s, the Midi contemplated electrifying the line, at that time comprising three or four mixed trains daily. In 1939, railcars took over. After the war, SNCF studied the possibility of putting express railcars from Millau to Nimes via Le Vigan, but — hardly surprisingly — the financial assessment was negative. Under SNCF's regional structure, the swansong of the steam-hauled freight on the eastern section was the arrival of ex-PLM 2-8-0s from Nimes running via Sommières and Le Vigan; but the writing was on the wall. In the spring of 1952, the section of line between L'Hospitalet-du-Larzac and Aveze-Moliéres was closed, and lifted three years later. The year 1955 saw the closure of the line between Tournemire and L'Hospitalet, although the track was left *in situ* at the request of the military authorities, who had training facilities in the wild and uninhabited terrain. Finally, the stub of line from Le Vigan to Aveze-Moliéres, served via the former PLM track from Nimes, was abandoned too. It seemed that the old Larzac line was to be obliterated for ever. However, unexpectedly, the military, with possession of the plateau between Tournemire-Roquefort and L'Hospitalet-du-Larzac, began to resettle and relay the track with their own railway specialists and motive power. By 1980, the track again reached L'Hospitalet. However, controversy erupted. My French informant — who remains anonymous! — describes events at 'La guerre du Larzac'. He concludes: 'The peasants having won, it was left unfinished.'

Eastwards from Le Vigan, the current SNCF freight atlas shows the line as still open for freight. Certainly when we were there, in 1981, the track was *in situ*, Le Vigan evidently still rail-connected, and all the signs existed of an active railway. Latest information is that the line from Le Vigan to Ganges (see map) is now closed, as the cost of bridge repairs was too high. However, Ganges to Quissac is still open 'provisionally'. Unofficially, if the Pennaroya Mine were to close, so would the line. Passengers are still carried by SNCF — by road.

The temptation indefinitely to describe an endless stream of crosscountry French railway lines and the policies that sustain them is strong. That the branch line to small towns like Bagnères de Bigorre, Sarrancolin, Luchon or Saint-Girons survive is remarkable (see the map on page 104). That the edifices and infrastructure remain not only intact

Above *I do not know when a passenger train last called here, but our visit was certainly memorable. . . 'Railway tourism' in France has endless possibilities.*

Opposite *Morning after the night before at what remains of the wayside station of Coulon. The station, a couple of miles from the village that bears its name, appears to be occupied by what might euphemistically be termed 'travellers' — but not by train! We are looking northwest, towards Fontenay-le-Comte some 15 miles away. Note the sharply-curved siding, which ran into a field.*

Table 388 (SNCF Ouest) covers, by Autocar, the Fontenay-Niort route by road. Thus Coulon still appears in an SNCF timetable, albeit a route based on the N148 rather than on steel rails.

Undulating rails disappearing into the distance illustrate the unlikely survival of lines through the countryside, such as this in Deux-Sèvres. On rural branch-lines from which passenger services have been withdrawn, SNCF sells the station buildings, even though the line still carries freight traffic.

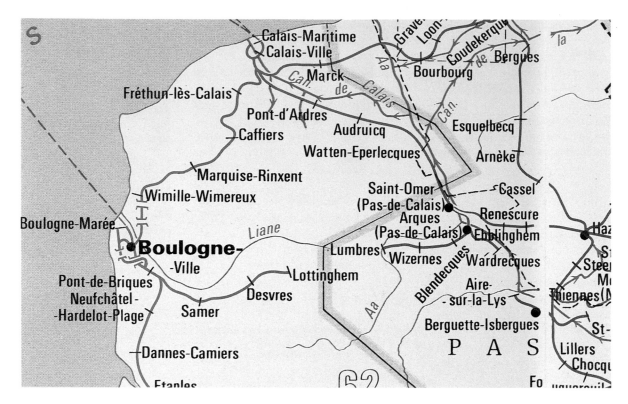

The cement works by Lumbres Station, seen opposite, can be located on the map above. Severing of cross-country lines has taken place all over France, but the stubs or longer branches remain intact if there is freight traffic. SNCF can thus legitimately assess operating costs, for sharing with local authority and/or commercial customers. Reference to this line is made on page 118.

but well maintained is both a compliment to France and a reprimand to ourselves.

Boussens to St-Girons, a distance of 32 km, boasts a thrice-weekly freight service on Monday, Wednesday and Friday. A small diesel shunter is stationed permanently at St-Girons, which lost its passenger service in 1969. The maintenance of the freight service, together with the retention of the splendid stations at these termini, helps SNCF to maintain a bus service with some style and dignity, where pick-up and set-down for bus passengers is easy in the ample space provided. The commitment of SNCF to their 'Autocar' services sees them included — indeed, almost indistinguishable from rail services — within the full regional timetables; see for example Table 438 on page 104.

So comprehensive is the inclusion of information at the station that, at St-Girons, Jane came rushing back to the car where I was changing film in a camera to hustle me on to the platform to record the arriving train. Fumbling furiously, I then raced through the station concourse, out on to the platform and away down its considerable length to await my photographic opportunity. Five, ten, fifteen minutes elapsed. Finally, at the distant station building — I had wandered off the end of the platform by this time — I saw that Jane was waving her arms to attract my attention and recall me. She had discovered that it was 18 years since the last passenger train arrival, and she had been reading the SNCF 'Autocar' timetable!

At Lannemezan, junction for the branch to Sarrancolin, which maintains a twice-weekly freight service, the overall roof sets off a stylish station kept spick and span by staff with pride in their railway. The arrival and departure of the 13.38 train to Lourdes was an *occasion*: the staff perform with panache.

This book is sponsored neither by SNCF nor by the French National Tourist Office; but to gastronomically-inclined Francophile railway enthusiasts, the Hautes-Pyrénées in early autumn, before the snow and the tourists arrive, is most agreeable. Let me finally, and for no particular reason, end this vignette on two other lines in another part of France: let us travel firstly to the Atlantic coast, to La Rochelle. From here, a comprehensive main line service runs north to Nantes, south to Bordeaux and north-east to Niort, Poitiers and Paris. Autorail services on regional routes and local stopping services, as well as autocar services to Velluise, complement the main line expresses. Marans, a village on the line to Nantes, enjoys the occasional train and the Autocar (see the maps on pages 110-1).

From Niort runs yet another single-track cross-country branch line,

'At Lumbres, west of St Omer on the erstwhile, but now severed, line to Boulogne, the large cement-works remains rail-connected.' (See page 118). On the day of my visit in September 1989, M Boyer was standing in for the stationmaster who was on holiday. In addition to serving the needs of Cement D'Ongry, the station still provides information about, and a booking-office for, SNCF services nation-wide. There is some road freight, but the bulk of the cement leaves the village by rail, often with three fully-laden trains per day.

207   RAPPEL : Ⓐ Tous les jours sauf samedis, dimanches et fêtes. Ⓑ Tous les jours sauf samedis. Ⓒ Samedis, dimanches et fêtes.   **207**

Boulogne-Ville ■━━━━━━━━━━━━━━━━━━━━━━━━■ Desvres

Identification		404	406	
Qualité		AUTOCAR	AUTOCAR	
Places assises		2	2	
Particularités				
Circulation		Ⓐ	Ⓐ	

Tab	Km		Origine	■	■	
	0	**Boulogne-Ville**		15 33	17 48	
	5	Pont-de-Briques	⊙	15 43	17 58	
	9	**Hesdigneul**	A	15 50	18 05	
		Hesdigneul		15 50	18 05	
	12	Carly	⊙	15 55	18 10	
	15	Samer	⊙	16 00	18 15	
	22	Longfosse	⊙	16 08	18 23	
	24	**Desvres**	◈ A	16 12	18 27	
		Terminus		■	■	

Identification		405	407	
Qualité		AUTOCAR	AUTOCAR	
Places assises		2	2	
Particularités				
Circulation		Ⓐ	Ⓐ	

Tab	Km		Origine	■	■	
	0	**Desvres**	◈	6 40	7 40	
	2	Longfosse	⊙	6 46	7 46	
	9	Samer	⊙	6 54	7 54	
	12	Carly	⊙	6 59	7 59	
	15	**Hesdigneul**	A	7 04	8 04	
		Hesdigneul		7 04	8 04	
	19	**Pont-de-Briques**	⊙ A	7 11	8 11	
	24	**Boulogne-Ville**	A	7 21	8 21	
		Terminus		■	■	

typical of the French railway scene, to terminate at Fontenay-le-Comte. Well off the tourist routes, in the station forecourt at what is now the line's terminus, stands a splendid *pissoir* of 'Clochmerle' dimensions.

The tracks which now terminate at Fontenay once ran north-westwards, to Chantonnay and Cholet. Services on this line ran separately from the Fontenay-Niort service; indeed, a study of the time-tables of 50 years ago, looked at alongside the current freight lines still open, indicates the sensible compromise of French railway policy. Cholet to Niort by rail is available, whilst communities on the erstwhile rural through line, Cholet-Chantonnay-Fontenay-Niort, are served by stubs of line once on this through route (see map). Time to explore the lifted sections, and to scavenge for souvenirs, might be more rewarding than in Britain, where we enthusiasts, locust-like, have combed the countryside.

One of the most sensible features of French railway policy is centred around the deliberate maintenance of freight services, often on remote rural branch-lines, in order to keep to a minimum the number of heavy lorries disturbing the peace and destroying unsuitable lanes. This is often done for one large customer — a quarry, a mine, or a cement-works. At Lumbres, west of St Omer on the erstwhile, but now severed, line to Boulogne, the large cement-works remains rail-connected. East of Boulogne the line remains intact to Desvres, whence a tourist passenger service has now been started (see above).

Sadly, and unlike Ordnance Survey, the Michelin maps do not indicate the tracks of disused railways. However, for the real flavour of the French branch line, let me recommend a visit, in the early morning, to the disused station of Coulon. More than a mile from the village that bears its name — where an excellent dinner and overnight stop may be enjoyed — a level crossing of the line by the D125 minor road provides the unforgettable atmosphere of the country railway. If you cannot enjoy the silence; the glinting sun on the undulating but dead-straight tracks disappearing in both directions; the empty wine bottles on the picnic-tables on the disused station platform; then you cannot appreciate France. If you are one such person, you are to be pitied...
Vive la France!

6
DECLINE IN STANDARDS

From an enjoyable Gallic ramble, it is time to return to the harsh reality of Britain's railways — or to be more specific, to British Railways, as in 1948 the newly-created monolith struggled to create a viable transport system from the ravages of war, the vicissitude of upheaval, the fragmentation of old loyalties.

The early years of the nationalized railway were dominated as much, if not more, by the ambitions, prejudices, and partial affections of powerful individuals as had been the Big Four railways from which the state system emerged. Indeed, without the discipline of Boards of Directors responsible to shareholders, the influence of the men at the top was probably greater. In no sphere of railway operation was this more evident than in the motive power policy. It is to the ambitions of Robert Arthur Riddles — Robin to his close friends — that we now turn our attention.

In a nutshell, Riddles was a steam man, weaned by the London & North Western Railway and matured by the LMS. As with all true railwaymen, and in contradistinction to many of those subsequently appointed to top positions by politicians and their protégés, Riddles' knowledge of his trade was born of personal experience, and equally important, of personal contact with the men who ran the railway. It seems unnecessary to say, but he would have deemed it unthinkable to have made decisions without close, frequent and deep consultation with the drivers and firemen who had to make his engines work. I enjoyed the privilege of a lengthy conversation with Riddles at his home in Calne, Wiltshire, in February 1981. He was in his 90th year, and it was some 2½ years before his death.

Joining the LNWR in 1909 as a premium apprentice at Crewe, Riddles quickly made his mark. His keen mind, willingness to learn and easy manner were moulded by those around him. The exchange trials of 1910, which brought Churchward's 'Star' Class 4-6-0 No 4005 *Polar Star* to Crewe, were to leave a lasting impression on the 18-year-old. In the following year, during the strike, he had his first taste of life on the footplate, all the 'premiums' and pupils being invited so to do by LNWR management. His resultant notes, relating the difficulty of shovelling coal through the firebox door of a 'Precedent' Class 2-4-0,

illustrate his concern not only for practical matters relating to efficiency, but also to the requirements of the men on the footplate.

Soon thereafter, war service was followed by a return to the LNWR, but at Rugby as a fitter, something of a demotion for the erstwhile Royal Engineers officer. The year 1919 brought another strike, Riddles again on the footplate, followed by confrontation with the union. This time he answered charges of attempted strike-breaking with an angry outburst that whilst they had been on strike for more pay, he and his comrades had been facing death in France due to lack of ammunition. He sought transfer from Rugby to Crewe in a letter to H.P.M. Beames, the Works Manager. This was granted, and ere long Beames recognized his ability. Promotion came quickly and, when Beames succeeded Bowen Cooke as Chief Mechanical Engineer, he put Riddles in charge of all locomotive building. One week later, at the turn of the year 1920-21, the erstwhile fitter from Rugby became assistant to the Works Manager.

Events moved quickly. In 1922, the LNWR merged with the Lancashire & Yorkshire; the following year, 1923, the Grouping — precursor to nationalization a quarter of a century later — saw the creation of the LMS. As a young man, Riddles was on the move within the fledgling new company. Sent to Horwich, he found many of the L & Y practices superior to LNWR ways. In spite of opposition from Beames to his proposed changes — opposition which in its early years bedevilled the LMS as former LNWR, L & Y and Midland men sought the pre-eminence of their chosen methods — Riddles was able to introduce changes which although detailed and related to locomotive repairs procedures, were successfully adopted and retained.

The General Strike of 1926 saw Riddles on the footplate yet again. This time, the length of the strike gave him a baptism of fire. Driving *Prince of Wales* Class 4-6-0 and *George the Fifth* Class 4-4-0 locomotives gave him a practical opportunity to assess the virtues and values of the differing wheel-arrangements. He himself says that this experience demonstrated the additional adhesion obtained by extra driving wheels — an experience which, in later years, assured his determination to press for a 2-10-0 rather than a 2-8-2 for heavy freight duty. Thus his early career, and subsequent rise through the LMS, plus his years at the War Department, influenced his decision to seek to build the BR Standard classes.

Loyalty to tried and trusted formulae, aligned to 'the company' and its works, plus personal loyalty to one's colleagues were determinant, not to say dominant, features of the scenario under which Riddles assumed his position. However, it is currently fashionable to criticize Riddles on two main counts: firstly that he sought to transpose 'LMS ways' to 'BR ways', and secondly that the decision to perpetuate the construction of new steam classes was not only a disaster, it was *his* disaster.

We have already seen (page 29) that the moves to form what became the Railway Executive Committee, in 1912, resulted from proposals emanating from the main pre-grouping companies — the LNWR, GWR, MR, GNR, GCR and LSWR. Co-ordinating their response to a perceived threat of war, they deduced that the railways would be best served by moving towards and co-operating with the ideas of Government, through legislation that had been on the statute book for more than 40 years. With the election of the Labour Government of 1945, the successors of those railway companies, the Big Four, were in a diametrically opposite mood and position from the situation pertaining in 1912. Where there had been a threat of war, there was now peace at the end of the war. Where there had been a perceived external threat, there was none. Where there had been relevant legislation on the statute book, there was none. Where there had been co-operation, there was hostility. This was the background to the events leading up to the creation of British Railways.

To this climate of hostility must be added other equally unpropitious factors: a railway system exhausted by war, yet still burdened with obligations faced by none of its competitors; a nation physically damaged and emotionally drained by that war; and four railway companies run by men steeped in the traditions and rivalries of their own separate experience. Under these circumstances, the criticisms levelled today at Riddles, by armchair critics with the benefit of hindsight, need to be seen in perspective. To those who say he should have abandoned steam and charged in, feet first, with diesel and electrification, I would humbly and briefly make two points, to which we shall return in more

Opposite *Although not officially one of the family of BR Standard locomotives, the War Department (WD) 'Austerity' engines, designed for service on the Western Front in the Second World War, need to be included in this chapter. Like the Standards, they were built to Riddles' designs, but introduced during the war — in 1943 to be precise — thus, of course, pre-dating the nationalization of the railways. Utility rather than style was their hallmark, as can be seen in this shot of 2-8-0 No 90111 at March on 4 February 1964.*

Based mechanically on the Stanier '8F', they had slightly larger diameter cylinders, and larger tenders. Out of a total of nearly 1,000 built by the North British Locomotive Co and Vulcan Foundry, 733 were purchased by BR from the Ministry of Supply. Twenty-five WD 2-10-0s which, with one exception, spent their BR days at work in Scotland, were also purchased by BR in 1948, of the 150 that had been built by the NB Locomotive Company. Rugged and reliable, they form an important, if unglamorous, part of the standardization story, designed by Riddles as Deputy Director-General of Royal Engineer Equipment.

The first of the 2-8-0s to be withdrawn was No 90083, taken out of service from March shed in December 1959; this photograph at the windswept Cambridgeshire depot was taken after it had officially closed. Lime-scaled No 90111 survived for another two months.

depth shortly. On electrification — where was the money to have come from? On dieselization — how much more chaotic would a crash programme thereof have been in 1948 than it was even when it was started, some years later? Riddles' task was to get the railways back on their feet, and steam was his chosen vehicle — reliable, trusty, well-understood steam. Indeed, the early BR diesels hardly became models of reliability and success.

As if the twin problems of hostility to the concept of nationalization and exhaustion born of war were not themselves sufficient, Riddles faced 'internal' as well as 'external' pressures that would have daunted a lesser man. These pressures can be encapsulated in four words: Churchward, Gresley, Stanier, Bulleid. Whilst only the last-mentioned was actually still in charge of affairs, as CME of the Southern, the legacy of and the successors to the traditions of the other three were factors, both in personality and practice, which presented Riddles with perhaps his greatest challenge, although of course as an LMS man much influenced by Stanier and H. G. Ivatt, it was really the GWR, LNER and SR regimes with which he had to cope. Indeed, his tussles with Bulleid about which he was so frank with me in my talk with him at Calne, caused him perhaps his greatest anguish.

Whilst illustratively Riddles is best remembered for his locomotives — and it is no part of my intention to detract from that aspect of his work — he does at least deserve to be credited with the tackling of fundamental organizational problems. As one simple example, he had to reconcile the practice of the GWR and LMS, where responsibility for locomotive construction and maintenance, carriage and wagon construction and maintenance and electrical engineering had all been the responsibility of the Chief Mechanical Engineer, whilst on the LNER and SR there had been a Chief Electrical Engineer. Again, unlike a 'normal' CME, he had no chief draughtsman, and not one but four drawing offices for locomotives, and four for carriages and wagons. Chief draughtsmen were not exactly humble and reticent by nature, either. In these circumstances, it is not only railway enthusiasts but anyone with an appreciation of the task facing Riddles who would take issue with critics like Dr Stewart Joy, who wrote, in *The Train That Ran Away*, so scathingly of Riddles' decision to build his new Standard classes.

Dr Joy accuses Riddles of 'an almost orgiastic relationship between man and machine', and poses the simplistic question, as a comment, that 'Either diesel traction was better than steam or it was not'. He seeks to crucify Riddles' reputation by referring to 'the personal ambitions of the successor to Stephenson, Webb, Churchward, Gresley and Stanier, who wished to design *his* own fleet of steam locomotives'. He justifies this calumny by comparing the situation in Britain with the contemporary scene in North America. Perhaps he overlooked the minor differences in the effects of the war and its aftermath on the financial and physical climate pertaining in a country that entered the war in 1939 and was but 22 miles from the nearest *Wehrmacht* and

Luftwaffe bases, with the financial and physical climate in a country that profited handsomely from Britain's plight in 1939-41, and whose citizens knew about the war at that time only from their newspapers and radios.

There is a more realistic assessment, in a simple sentence in the introduction to *BR Standard Steam in Close-Up* by Tony Fairclough and Alan Wills, who state: 'However, following Nationalization in January 1948 it was decided by the newly-formed Railway Executive that because of the economic climate, steam would have to continue as the main-stay for some years to come and that it would be politic to develop new locomotives which were not too obviously based upon any one of the original "Big Four" types, as this would have smacked of favouritism and been the source of possible friction between the Regions.'

To find a dispassionate assessment in the 'steam v diesel' argument is not so easy. Riddles' critics, and indeed critics of the decision to build the Standard steam classes, conveniently forget the disappointment, [...] disaster that attended the early [...]isation Plan. Frequent failures [...]ffic. Inadequate weight on, for [...] Type '2', causing lack of braking [...] North British Loco 1000/1200 [...]ications required by the English

Classified '3' and designed for light passenger work, the '82xxx' 2-6-2Ts would, with the benefit of hindsight, never have been built. Soon after they, and the lighter Class '2' 2-6-2T '84xxx's arrived on the scene, diesel multiple or single units were making their presence felt. Unlike the '2' 2-6-2Ts, however, there was no pre-nationalization model which could be repeated.

Whilst dieselization and line closures displaced these neat tank engines from their original haunts, they made a welcome appearance in London, themselves replacing aged 'M7' tanks on empty stock workings into Waterloo. Here, on 26 March 1964, No 82014, with Bulleid coaches in tow, sets off for Clapham carriage sidings as my commuter train approaches the terminus.

ERRATA

* The photographs (though not the captions) on pages 125 and 169 are transposed.

* The caption on page 150 should commence with the word 'Below' not 'Opposite'.

Electric 'Baby Deltics', with availability so poor that at one stage in the spring of 1962 only two were in traffic, with failure being endemic — the story was hardly one of glorious success. Unfashionable as it may be to say so, the Western Region's diesel-hydraulic locomotives were more reliable but, as successors to the GWR, the Region's unilateral decision to opt for diesel-hydraulic, rather than diesel-electric, was not tolerated by a system hell-bent on uniformity. Thus the Swindon-built 'Warships' that gave excellent service, the reliable 'Hymeks', and the — by diesel standards — stylish 'Westerns' had to go. Had you asked a shedmaster in 1959 if he would prefer an NBL Type '2' or a BR Standard Class '5' 4-6-0, the answer in terms of reliability if not of direct comparability would not have been in much doubt.

Hindsight can be wonderfully convenient as a means of justifying one's criticism of the decisions and events of yesteryear. As BR in 1989 struggles to overcome the mechanical problems of its 'Pacer' diesel units, perhaps Dr Joy should tell us *which* diesels Riddles should have recommended in 1948. Should we have imported them, within the climate of financial crisis that so dominated our lives in Britain, from the USA? His book was written in 1973. He failed to quote in it some significant figures relating to initial costs as between steam, diesel and electric locomotives that were current in 1950, and which are extracted from Col Rogers biography of Robin Riddles, *The Last Steam Locomotive Engineer.*

Type	Capital Cost	Starting tractive effort (TE) (lbs)	Cost per lb of TE (converted to decimal currency)	Drawbar horsepower (DBHP)	Cost per DBHP
BR Class '5' 4-6-0	£16,000	26,120	61½p	1,200	£13.30
1,600 hp Diesel-electric	£78,000	41,400	£1.89	1,200	£65.00
2,500 hp Gas turbine	£138,700	33,000	£4.20	2,000	£69.35
Co-Co electric 1,500 volts	£37,400	45,000	84p	2,120	£17.68

These figures, shown baldly thus, may be considered to be selective. As Peter Semmens, in checking my manuscript, has pointed out, they overlook the steam locomotive's inability to generate its maximum power for a lot of the time; nor do they take account of the efficiency of modern electrics and diesels, which reduce their running costs and increase their availability. But the 1948 beggar was not the 1988 chooser, and the figures in my chart stand on their own.

Seeking to judge the validity of the view of Riddles' critics, and faced with these figures, one cannot fail to be reminded of Marie Antoinette's celebrated advice to the bread-starved citizenry. Perhaps, from my own distant memories, I can cull the discussions amongst contemporary womenfolk about the shortage of nylon stockings. Of course, the virtues and values of diesel and/or electric motive power were discussed and fully appreciated. The Chairman of the British Transport Commission, Sir Cyril (later Lord) Hurcomb, had called for an *economic* assessment of diesel and electric traction in April 1948. Its content is well-enough known, and the report, submitted in October 1951, recommended extensive experiments with main line diesel and electric traction. But, in the meantime, Riddles and his team had to keep the show on the road. In the time the committee took to produce its report, the 'Britannia' 4-6-2s, Standard Class '5' 4-6-0s, Class '4' 4-6-0s and Class

Opposite *Paucity of material — this is, I think, my only photograph of a BR Standard '2' 2-6-2T — accounts for the inclusion of this photograph, of No 84002 out of steam inside Bletchley MPD on 28 April 1963, some two years before withdrawal. Unusually — indeed uniquely amongst the 30 locomotives in the '84xxx' Class — she spent her last eight years allocated to the same shed.*

Little has been written about this small class, probably because, due to their similarity to Ivatt's LMS design of 1946, there is little original to be said. With Riddles' LMS background and his close affinity to and with Ivatt, his '2' 2-6-2T would, were it not for railway politics and the need to create 'new' standard classes, have been accommodated by a repeat order for the Ivatt machines.

Indeed, production of the Ivatt 2-6-2T was continued by BR until 1952, and these Riddles engines superseded them in 1953, when the first 20 were built. The final 10, Nos 84020-84029, were built in 1957; No 84012 was withdrawn in 1963. The class were motor-fitted for push and pull working.

'4' 2-6-4Ts had been designed — at Derby, Doncaster, Brighton and Brighton respectively — and already introduced. Whilst Riddles was in effect — if not in name — CME of British Railways, it was E.S. Cox in practice who was the design supremo who saw his chief's policy translated into actual locomotives. Cox was an LMS man, formerly from the Lancashire & Yorkshire Railway; his partner under Riddles was Roland C. Bond, another LMS man, who became Chief Officer (Locomotive Construction and Maintenance).

Before we look at the locomotives themselves, however, we need, again, to remind ourselves of the economic climate of the day, during those troubled years immediately succeeding the war. It is certainly no part of my intention to pontificate about the success or otherwise of the economic policies pursued by the Attlee Government. Discussion about the merits of large-scale electrification with its inherent capital costs, or the purchase of off-the-shelf diesel locomotives from the United States, can only take place against an informed assessment of the economic situation. The benefits to our exporters arising from the disequilibrium of the dollar-sterling balance of payments was, *per se*, an enormous obstacle to the ambitions of importers, even for essential goods. This was aggravated by the convertibility crisis of 1947. There was a drastic drain on our gold and dollar reserves. Nationalization was expensive, and — rightly or wrongly, I do not comment — was seen overseas as putting political theory before economic necessity. Marshall Aid seemed to give us a new chance of recovery in 1948 — the first year of railway nationalization — but by the summer of 1949 another, and more acute, balance of payments crisis led to further cuts in dollar imports. The pound was heavily devalued on 18 September that year, and simultaneously HMG announced further drastic internal economies aimed at reducing current spending and capital expenditure. And whilst our private sector locomotive builders were, it is true, building some diesels for export, they were not in any way suitable for a BR system whose motive power infrastructure was wholly extant for the steam era at that time.

At the 1950 General Election, Labour just held on to office. Soon thereafter, the oil crisis in Persia involving the Anglo-Iranian oil installations might, in retrospect and with the benefit of hindsight, have made people thankful that our railway system was not then dependent on oil supplies for its operation. If all this seems an irrelevant glimpse into distant history, before such phrases as 'North Sea Oil' had been invented, do remember that these could have been vital factors if the Riddles Standard locomotives had not been under construction. Meanwhile, the balance of payments situation worsened yet again...

In 1951, a Conservative Government was returned to office, albeit, like its Labour predecessor in the 1950 election, one with a small majority. At the time of the election the incoming Government was faced with yet another major economic crisis. The gold and dollar reserves were fast dwindling and there was talk of the threat of national bankruptcy. By the date of the next election in 1955, however, the economic scene was very much improved — road transport had been de-nationalized and the Persian oil crisis was resolved. On the transport front, the incoming Conservative Government of 1951 had abandoned Labour's idea of 'integration' under a public monopoly. The duties of the BTC were redefined, and the railways were released from some of their burdensome and restrictive statutory obligations in the Transport Act of 1953. In due course there followed the 1955 Modernisation Plan, and the intended elimination of steam.

It is important to emphasize that changed attitudes to steam, between 1948 and 1953, were due as much to this fundamental change in the economic affairs of the nation as to any other factor. Thus, with hindsight, to blame Robin Riddles, as has been done in some quarters, whilst ignoring the environment in which his decision, and that of the BTC, was made, is, in my view, quite inappropriate and unfair. Let us now have a look at his locomotives, and then we can assess the merits or otherwise of the decision which resulted in engines being scrapped in their working infancy.

'Manchester and Liverpool were gradually rising in importance and increasing in population.....' It was the east-west links 'twixt city and port that were the catalyst for Manchester's first railways. The great linked stations of Victoria and Exchange housed the longest railway station platform in Britain. By 24 June 1968 steam had but six weeks left on BR's tracks, but Standard Class '5' 4-6-0 No 73050, seen here entering Victoria Station, survived into preservation. Her '9H' shedplate indicates a Patricroft-based locomotive, one of the once numerous steam depots in and around Manchester.

Excepting the unique '8P' Duke of Gloucester, the most powerful and largest of the express passenger locomotives amongst the Standard classes were the 'Britannia' 'Pacifics', 55 of which were built. Although they worked on principal express duties on all regions except the North Eastern, they gradually gravitated to the London Midland Region, and by 1963 most were allocated to LMR sheds. On 28 April that year, No 70012 John of Gaunt and No 70042 Lord Roberts, both allocated at that date to Willesden (1A), were heading north on the West Coast Main Line.

The scene on today's electrified West Coast Main Line here at Bletchley could hardly be more different. The sight of two 'Pacifics' simultaneously departing would rightly be nothing but a dream.

Perhaps the first point to make about the locomotives themselves is that they are known as *the* Standards. Whereas an 'A4' has the adjectival prefix 'Gresley', the 'Merchant Navy' Bulleid, the 28xx 'Churchward', the 'Riddles' prefix is rarely attached to 'his' engines. Indeed, Riddles himself was the first to ascribe due credit to his colleagues concerned in BR with locomotive affairs. Men of stature, competence, ability and experience surrounded him, men whose names have properly earned their due public accolade in the last few years. The two most prominent, already mentioned, were Roland C. Bond and E.S. Cox, and, like Riddles, they were former LMS men. Behind them were the Chief Draughtsmen in the pre-nationalization 'Company' drawing offices, which themselves were to share in the development of the new designs. At Derby, J.W. Caldwell, in charge of what was now the BR Regional Drawing Office there, took responsibility for the 'Britannia' 'Pacifics', for the sole '8P Pacific' *Duke of Gloucester*, for the 'Clan' Class 'Pacifics', for the Class '2' 2-6-0 and the Class '2' 2-6-2T. At Doncaster, E. Windle was responsible for the Class '5' 4-6-0 and the Class '4' 2-6-0. (Why, one muses, was the Class '5', with its LMS/Stanier antecedence, not done at Derby?) At Swindon, F.C. Mattingley, of many years' experience, may have felt demeaned by responsibility only for the Class '3' 2-6-0 and Class '3' 2-6-2T, a total of 65 engines only actually being built. At Brighton, C.S. Cocks, joined later by R.G. Jarvis, had charge not only of the Class '4' 4-6-0 and the 2-6-4T, but also the truly outstanding '9F' 2-10-0.

Thus were the tasks involved in designing the Standards spread amongst the Regional Drawing Offices, one each from the erstwhile GWR, LMS, LNER and SR. To those who believe that there were always two railways in Britain, namely the Great Western and The Rest, it was undoubtedly regarded as a deliberate snub that Swindon's role was so small. Yet, with Riddles charged with the task of eliminating any 'cult of the personality' from the austere nationalized structure, perhaps the ghost of Churchward had to be exorcized.

To separate any assessment of each of the 12 Standard classes from the tasks which they were designed to perform is futile: like anything mechanical, they were essentially functional, built to undertake a clearly-defined task. Furthermore, the assessment of each class must be related to the demand for the motive power for which each was designed. Thus, when the 'Britannias' appeared in 1951 there was a demand for express passenger motive power, whilst, albeit only two years later, there really was little need for a new class '2' 2-6-2 tank engine. This was a reflection of the fact that diesel multiple units were soon to come on stream to handle cross-country and branch line duties, whilst there was, as yet, no wholesale production of main line diesel locomotives to haul the main passenger trains. Assessment, therefore, of the Standard classes needs to be made in the light of the prevailing motive power situation on BR in the first decade after the Second World War.

Two main questions in this look at the Standard locomotives might

On 9 July 1967, double-chimneyed Standard '4' 4-6-0 No 75075 sticks her graffiti-covered smokebox out of Nine Elms MPD on the very last day of operation at that famous place, now covered with the faceless concrete laughingly called 'New Covent Garden'. She was withdrawn at the end of the day, gloomily recorded by the chalk messages.

Eighty of these useful and successful mixed-traffic locomotives were built — at Swindon, where failures were rare. Lack of light did not help when taking photographs like this.

usefully, if not originally, be addressed. Firstly, why was it necessary to design any new locomotives when each of the Big Four had more than adequate motive power designs for its own requirements, on tap and indeed often under construction? Secondly, how did the new locomotives compare, and how were they perceived to compare, with the 'Company' motive power alongside and in replacement of which they were to work?

Undoubtedly, railway politics lay at the heart of the answer to the first question, as well as the need to make a start on the creation of uniform, interchangeable motive power. If one can cast one's mind back to 1948 and try to imagine the resistance and resentment of the old companies to the change that was thrust upon them, adding insult to injury was to be avoided at all costs. In today's world of HSTs operating from Paddington, St Pancras and King's Cross, the idea of different motive power based on history and tradition, rather than uniformity based on interchangeability and economy of operation, would seem extravagant, not to say bizarre. In the fledgling years of BR, however, it was a very different scene.

Furthermore, many of the 'Company' locomotives were not only modern but still in production. Once it had been decided to build a new fleet of 'Standard' steam locomotives, it was probably essential, if *esprit de corps* was to be generated, to go in for new designs, a new image, a new breed. Bear in mind that nationalization was a 'political' decision, and therefore 'railway politics' were an essential ingredient in top management decision-making.

Turning now to the second question, namely comparisons and perception, it should be stressed that if the Standards were 'political' in concept, they were purely practical in production. Riddles and his team, strapped into an economic straitjacket within a railway-political minefield (excuse the mixed metaphors!) came to the obvious conclusion that 'Ivatt Ugliness' was better than 'Bulleid Complexity': in other words, the ease of maintenance concomitant with high running plates was an attraction, whereas the idiosyncrasy of Bulleid's chain-driven valve gear was not.

The views of the railwaymen presented with their new steeds inevitably related to their current circumstances. Thus on the Great Eastern main line from Liverpool Street, a 'Britannia', albeit a larger and more powerful locomotive, was a godsend as replacement for a 'B1' on express duty; but on the Western, the new engines found little favour with men at home on the footplate of a 'King' or a 'Castle'. Lower down the scale, there were some men, such as Bath Green Park's crews, who seemed to prefer their Standard '5' 4-6-0s to their Stanier 'Black Fives'; but my impression, gained in discussions at the time and in retrospect, is that most crews found little, if any, advantage to driving or firing the Standards when compared to the Stanier machines.

Entitled 'Decline in Standards', this chapter draws to its close by lamenting the comparatively short working lives of the Riddles machines, if they may be thus described *in memoriam*. Whether or not they were capable, or indeed whether the steam locomotive itself, dating from the Stephenson era, was capable of much further 'technological stretch' is a matter for engineers, not politicians. The Caprotti valve-gear fitted to the last 30 Class '5s' seems to have been successful, if slightly ugly. Even in those austere post-war days some concession was made to aesthetics. Research at Swindon into draughting indicated that a small diameter blast-pipe and chimney undoubtedly improved steam raising. The logical outcome was a narrow stove-pipe chimney. E.S. Cox, however, mindful of the reaction to Bulleid's 'Q1', decided that the narrow bore of the internal lining should be encased in a larger, traditional exterior. That the style of said casing would not have been totally unrecognizable to those weaned on the Lancashire & Yorkshire at Horwich some 30 years earlier was not unrelated to Cox's background on the L & Y before the LMS came into being. Such is railway life.

Thus it was the end of steam, not the obsolescence of the locomotives, that finished off the BR Standard classes. Many were freely transferred from one end of the country to another, as operating conditions dictated. For instance:

70020 from Cardiff Canton to Carlisle Kingmoor
73016 from Canklow to Eastleigh
75071 from Templecombe to Croes Newydd
76033 from March to Brighton
78032 from Chester (Midland) to Kirkby Stephen
80042 from Bletchley to Ashford
82027 from York to Guildford
84009 from Hull Dairycoates to Llandudno Junction
92001 from Tyseley to Wakefield

No mention has been made of the Riddles 'Austerity' locomotives which, it could be claimed, were the precursors of standardization, as indeed they were. In terms of creating a single unified national pattern for motive power, Riddles and his team were the trail-blazers. Arguments about whether a near-bankrupt system could have afforded or should have plunged straight into the mass introduction of diesel power have been briefly covered in this chapter. Suffice it to say that, in terms of creating, as he was bidden, a single, rather than a diverse, entity, Riddles' Standard engines fulfilled their role.

None did more so than the quite outstanding '9F' 2-10-0s. Much has been written about these superb machines. Introduced as recently as 1954, the last member of the class was built at Swindon and entered service in 1960. By 1964, the first '9F' was withdrawn: premeditated profligacy indeed. Riddles, designer of the 'Austerity' 2-10-0 built for the War Department, presided over the design and construction of a thoroughly modern locomotive — ten-coupled engines were very rare indeed before Riddles got to work. The deliberate decimation of motive power willing and able to provide years of service was inexcusable. There was no built-in obsolescence about the '9F'.

7
OUT OF STEAM

In 1958, British Railways had more than 16,000 standard gauge steam locomotives actively on its books including the growing ranks of Standards. By the end of August 1968 they had all gone. A handful survived into preservation; the remainder were deliberately destroyed, cut up either at various BR workshops or sold to and decimated by private contractors in their yards. Names such as Cashmore's, Bird's, Ward's, Cohen's, King's and, of course, Woodham's, are familiar to students of the subject.

To those without knowledge of railway matters, replacing obsolete locomotives may seem similar to replacing worn-out company trucks, vans or cars for a company manufacturing, selling and distributing washing-powder. Yet that is to equate Ford, General Motors, British Leyland or Honda with the Swindon, Eastleigh, Doncaster or Derby works of the GWR, SR, LNER and LMS. It would be hard to find a less apt, less accurate and less likely analogy.

Where the manufacturer of the internal combustion engine builds in obsolescence, the railway companies, and the 'outside' builders, built machines to last. Where the one went for fancy fashion, the other went for sturdy continuity. Where the one went for quantity, the other went for quality. Where the one was an anonymous 'multinational' of nameless, faceless 'executives', the other bore a direct, visible, personal connection to, and with, the 'end-user'. Whilst in the last chapter I was able to refer to Riddles, Bond, Cox *et al*, who is to be called to account for the design and performance of contemporary 'motive power' in the case of the Ford Consul, the Triumph Renown or the Jowett Javelin?

Thus, whilst there were bad steam engines, they were comparatively few and far between, certainly by the latter half of this century. The result, therefore, was that the successful locomotives lasted and multiplied. Consequently, many pre-war locomotives were performing efficiently, normally and quite unexceptionally into the 1960s, notwithstanding the standardization policy of the GWR which, more successfully and thoroughly than the other companies, replaced many of their old, non-standard locomotives with new builds. A 30-year-old locomotive was commonplace; a 40-year-old locomotive was interesting in that it probably pre-dated the 1923 Grouping when Baldwin's

Conservative Government deemed that the multiplicity of railway companies was creating an unacceptable level of wasteful competition; and a 50-year-old locomotive took us back to the first decade of this century. And yet, even in the 1960s, there were still at work, in normal revenue-earning service, engines designed and built in the Victorian era. On the Southern Region, 'M7' 0-4-4 tanks still performed, let alone the Beattie well tanks approaching their 90th birthday in Cornwall. At the other end of Britain, former North British Railway Class 'C' (latterly LNER Class 'J36') 0-6-0s, from a class introduced in 1888, still performed their duties undaunted.

In between these veterans, and the BR Standard classes, an army of utterly reliable steam engines kept the railways working. It is as a tribute to these ordinary workhorses that this chapter is dedicated. Naturally, geography dictated the locomotives that I was able to photograph in those final years, although certain classes, by their very numbers, were both widespread and common. The LMS 'Black Five' 4-6-0s and '8F' 2-8-0s, plus the ubiquitous GWR '57xx' 0-6-0 pannier tanks come to mind initially. On the Southern Region, Bulleid 'Pacifics' were,

On a dull Saturday afternoon in April 1963, my inquisitive nose discovered an antique at the back of Bedford shed. Already withdrawn the previous month and awaiting the final call to be scrapped at Derby Works was former Midland Railway Johnson '3F' 0-6-0 No 43453, survivor from a class introduced in 1885; certainly Beeching had real problems in his legacy of Victoriana. A kind foreman mobilized 'Black Five' No 45416 to heave this veteran from the dark recesses of the shed into the gloomy light, to enable me to capture her for posterity.

if not two-a-penny, sufficiently numerous as to evince no excitement.

As the end of steam approached, as the diesels and electrics multiplied, the sight of a steam engine — any steam engine — became an event. Once, during a three-hour vigil near Weston-super-Mare in July 1963, more than two years before the end of Western Region steam, I was rewarded with but one photograph. My catalogue illustrates with grisly clarity the steady diminution of variety between the end of November 1962 when my first colour photograph was taken, and that final week of steam, ending in August 1968, when even the 'Standards' had gone, and Stanier's 'Black Fives' and '8Fs' did the final honours. I have therefore set my hand to the daunting task of listing opposite all the different classes of locomotives that I managed to photograph in colour in that period, the last 5½ years of British steam.

Scrutiny of my catalogue of 'living steam' for cross-reference with the identical numbers of locomotives that ended their days at Barry, is an interesting task. If only in, say, 1965, just before the end of steam, one had known a) that Barry scrapyard existed, b) that fate would leave locomotives there for 15 or 20 years, and c) which ones would survive, one could have photographed those survivors whilst they were still in

Class	Introduced	Class	Introduced
LBSCR: A1	1872	GWR: 54xx	1931
LSWR: 0298	1874	GWR: 14xx	1932
MR: Johnson 3F 0-6-0	1885	LMS: Stanier 2-6-0	1933
NB: J36	1888	GWR: 72xx	1934
LSWR: 02	1889	LMS: Jubilee	1934
LSWR: B4	1891	LMS: 5	1934
LSWR: G6	1894	LMS: Stanier 2-6-4T	1935
LSWR: M7	1897	LMS: 8F	1935
LBSCR: E4	1897	LNER: A4	1935
LSWR: 700	1897	LNER: V2	1936
LSWR: T9	1899	GWR: Grange	1936
MR: 3F 0-6-0T	1899	LMS: Coronation	1937
LSWR: T9	1899	SR: Q	1938
GWR: 28xx	1903	GWR: Manor	1938
SECR: H	1904	SR: Merchant Navy	1941
LBSCR: E6	1904	SR: USA	1942
NER: J27	1906	SR: Q1	1942
GWR: 1361	1910	LNER: B1	1942
GWR: 43xx	1911	LMS: Rebuilt Royal Scot	1943
MR: 4F	1911	(BR): WD	1943
LBSCR: K	1913	GWR: Modified Hall	1944
NER: Q6	1913	LNER: O1	1944
S DJR: 7F	1914	LNER: O4/8	1944
SECR: N	1917	GWR: County	1945
GWR: 47xx	1919	LNER: A1	1945
LSWR: S15	1920	LMS: Fairburn 2-6-4T	1945
LSWR: H16	1921	SR: West Country	1945
GWR: Castle	1923	LNER: A2/3	1946
LMS: 3F 0-6-0T	1924	LMS: 2 2-6-2T	1946
GWR: Hall	1924	LMS: 2 2-6-0	1946
LMS: 4F	1924	SR: Battle of Britain	1946
LNER: K3/2	1924	LMS: Rebuilt Patriot	1946
GWR: 56xx	1924	LMS: 4 2-6-0	1947
LMS: 'Crab'	1926	GWR: 94xx	1947
LNER: A3	1927	GWR: 15xx	1949
GWR: 4575	1927	GWR: 16xx	1949
LMS: 2-6-4T	1927	BR: Britannia	1951
GWR: King	1927	BR: 4 2-6-4T	1951
SR: U	1928	BR: 5 4-6-0	1951
SR: U1	1928	BR: 4 4-6-0	1951
GWR: 5101	1929	BR: 3 2-6-2T	1952
GWR: 57xx	1929	BR: 2 2-6-0	1953
SR: V	1930	BR: 4 2-6-0	1953
GWR: 2251	1930	BR: 2 2-6-2T	1953
SR: W	1931	BR: 9F	1954
GWR: 61xx	1931		

Overleaf *Labour shortages, with unwillingness to work in the grimy surroundings of the steam shed, are epitomized by Southern Railway Maunsell 'S15' 4-6-0 No 30835, seen here at Redhill MPD in April 1963. The open door of the smokebox reminds us that cleaning out the ash and char was hot and choking work. Nevertheless, the rivets so clearly highlighted by the Perutz film in my £20 Voigtlander camera personify the durability of the steam engine, the demise of which has left an unashamedly irreplaceable gap in the landscape for railway enthusiasts.*

revenue-earning service with British Rail. But, such is life.

There is something excruciatingly painful in unearthing 'before-and-after' pictures of the same locomotive in 'alive' and 'dead' guise. Up until now, my books have included few photographs of withdrawn engines at their final BR resting places prior to cutting up. My stock of shots on this subject, in colour, is quite extensive, although 'colour' is not much in evidence when the subject is a withdrawn engine in a dank, grey siding at the back of a motive power depot. A random example is given in the table overleaf.

There are of course other duplicated 'in service' and 'at Barry' locomotives in my collection, but lack of space precludes their mention here. Whilst these five locomotives feature purely by chance, they do illustrate two points made earlier. Firstly, a good locomotive, ably fulfilling the role for which it was designed, as for example Urie's 'S15' Class originally built by the London & South Western Railway in 1920, were still at work 40 years later, still capably handling freight traffic. The

Forever associated with Wales and with South Wales in particular, were the GWR '56xx' Class 0-6-2Ts, introduced in 1924 for service in the Welsh valleys. The power and pugnacity of these Collett locomotives is self-evident even in decline, as here with No 5676 at Croes Newydd on 20 March 1966.

The bunker-side numberplate will have been taken into safe keeping by the shed's management or, quite likely, been stolen. Maintaining watch on portable items of BR property as sheds closed was well-nigh impossible.

Number	Class	Built	Withdrawn	Photographed		Left Barry	Current site
30499	'S15'	5/20	1/64	Basingstoke 8/63	Barry 1980 Barry 1982	1983	Mid Hants Railway
34058	'Battle of Britain'	3/47	10/64	Andover 8/63	Barry 1980	1986	Bitton Railway
75079	BR '4' 4-6-0	1/56	11/66	Eastleigh 5/63	Barry 1980	1982	Plym Valley Railway
31638	'U'	5/31	1/64	Redhill 6/63	Barry 1980	1980	Bluebell Railway
35027	'Merchant Navy'	12/48	9/66	Loco Junction, Nine Elms 5/63	Barry 1980	1982	Swindon-Cricklade Railway

The goods trains we knew and loved were still in evidence in the 1960s. On 25 June 1965, SR 'N' Class 2-6-0 No 31842 has steam to spare as she trundles along the South Western main line 'twixt Fleet and Winchfield. These Maunsell 'Moguls', introduced in 1917, gave sterling service, from Kent to Cornwall, on mixed traffic duties right across Southern Railway territory. The first members of the class were withdrawn in late 1962; by January 1965 only 12 remained, including No 31842 which went three months after this photograph was taken. She was scrapped at Cashmore's, Newport, in November that year.

same applies to Maunsell's 'Moguls', of which No 31842, seen in the accompanying photograph, is a typical example. Both classes seemed to epitomize the reliability, lack of fuss and honesty of purpose of the steam engine. Conversely, the life-span of the youngest of the quintet was a mere ten years, history and experience dictating beyond peradventure that scrapping after such a short life could be described as infanticide.

The Bulleid 'Pacifics', of which no fewer than 30 landed at Barry, were the last of the main line passenger steam locomotives to succumb to the cutter's torch, and thus feature in the chart; mathematically and geographically within the ambit of my own movements and the locations from which Dai Woodham purchased his locomotives, this is hardly surprising, as they were retained in active service until the completion of the Bournemouth line electrification.

The history of the locomotives that ended up as Dai Woodham's property has now been extensively recorded, emphasizing the widespread interest that exists in such a seemingly melancholy subject. Further-

The LMS, having pioneered diesel-powered locomotion in Britain with its diesel shunters, was determined to see its initials on the side of the nation's first main-line diesel-electric locomotives. The Chief Mechanical Engineer, H.G. Ivatt, was in charge of construction of 10000 and 10001, and the former was completed at Derby Works in December 1947, days before the end of the LMS and its assimilation into British Railways.

No 10001, seen here inside Willesden roundhouse in March 1963, survived in traffic until March 1966.

Previous page *In a book tracing the transition from 'old' to 'new' railway, the Ivatt LMS '4' 2-6-0 admirably epitomizes the quantum leap from style to practicality; from demure appearance in the era of cheap labour, to the post-war realism of approaching classlessness. With high running-plate and exposed motion for ease of maintenance, No 43021, from a class introduced in 1947 in the final year of the LMS before nationalization, shuffles past Watford Junction station, with recently erected catenaries portending the electric future. It is 14 May 1964.*

more, the story of the scrapping of the huge BR steam fleet has itself been recorded, numerically, photographically and historically. However, a brief examination of the saga of withdrawal, in some cases storage, de-coaling, dispatch to the hands of the scrapmen and ultimate dismemberment, is all part of the story of how Britain's railways were forced 'out of steam'.

As with other aspects of contemporary railway activity, the physical scrapping of the steam fleet, with its visually emotive scenes, was but a manifestation of the centralized decision-making of the nationalized railway system. If the Big Four had still comprised the commercial structure of our railways, would they all simultaneously have reached the same conclusion about the timing and method of introduction of new motive power?

Let us contemplate the imaginary board room discussions of, say, the LMS management at the appropriate agenda item:

'4. Motive Power Replacement Programme:

'H.G., would you like to open discussion on this item?'

Responding to the chairman's invitation, Ivatt might have proffered one of the following scenarios:

'Chairman, I have two alternative proposals: may I outline them briefly, and the board can discuss them.'

At this point, say in 1950, or whenever you choose, H.G. Ivatt unveils his chart of existing LMS motive power. He — briefly — reminds the Board of the technical advances of steam, diesel and electric traction, and the financial criteria to be considered.

'Without doubt, Chairman, the electric railway is the railway of the future, and the technology is available here and now. But the capital cost is high. With steam, my view is that technical developments are unlikely to do more than improve marginally the cost-efficiency of the machine, although we have a preponderance of reliable motive power, and continuing standardization is reducing our operating costs. The real problem is manpower, and growing resistance to the working conditions concomitant with the steam engine. Our experience with diesel power is limited in depth to our shunting locomotives, although they can do all that is demanded of them. Even so, we really have only a handful in the context of the total shunting activity performed on the railway. On the passenger side, our two Co-Co locomotives built at Derby are performing well enough, but it is far too soon to recommend replacing our steam fleet wholesale with diesels.'

'What about costs, H.G.?'

'Well, Chairman, the coal shortage a couple of years ago reminded us of our dependence on factors beyond our control. With coal or diesel we are in the hands of others. I suppose theoretically that is true of electricity, but supply and costs of electric power, now and in the future, can be prognosticated on the assumption that those in charge of producing the nation's electricity will themselves take advantage of supply costs and of advancing technology.'

'What are the London and North Eastern, Great Western and Southern up to? Are we missing out on anything?'

'Chairman, you are aware of the Southern's extensive pre-war electrification programme, although the war and the current economic climate have put a stop to any further advances. The Southern and the Western have barely dipped their toes into the diesel pond. At the moment, the only real operational experience with main line diesel power is across the Atlantic, but they have all the oil they need and their railways, frankly, were untouched by the war.'

H.G. Ivatt now outlines his plan for the future.

'Chairman, my outline for the future touches on the preserve of my operational colleagues, so let me restrict myself to general ideas and propositions. They are related to the state of our finances, the state of technical progress, and an assumption of trends in traffic patterns, not only on the LMS, but throughout the country. I think we should embark on extensive diesel trials with main line locomotives; plan to electrify the busiest lines; contemplate rationalizing our lines where there is an overlap, say, into high-speed passenger and express freight; and for the foreseeable future plan to continue to modernize and standardize our steam stock, whilst concentrating it on those services where speed is not the first priority. In other words, Chairman, let us look at our duplicated routes, categorize them into high-speed/new technology and lower-speed/existing technology routes, and provide motive power accordingly, within our resources.'

That is how it might have been: an orderly if controversial marriage of tradition and technology. But, of course, it was not at all like that. The 8,084 steam locomotives bequeathed by the LMS to British Railways on 1 January 1948 were the largest single contribution to a total steam fleet of 19,500 when British Railways was born, a product not of board room planning, but of political will. The merits and methods — or lack of — are discussed elsewhere in this book. With the birth of BR, political rather than commercial decisions, centralized and often regardless of circumstances, were the order of the day. Instead of a planned and phased policy of gradual change in the light of existing circumstances, we had a 'railway-political' decision to build a new generation of Standard steam locomotives rather than the concentration on, and of, existing types. This was to be followed, in the 1955 BR Modernisation Plan, of another 'railway-political' decision: scrap steam — fast, regardless of the usefulness of the fleet, without any thought of planned decline by route or traffic type.

The speed and scale of the task is illustrated by the chart overleaf of BR steam's last ten years, prepared by the Railway Correspondence and Travel Society (RCTS), an organization to which I have belonged for many years and to whom I gladly give credit.

As I write these words, in 1989, we are in the midst of a serious industrial dispute on BR. For the footplatemen's union, ASLEF, this chart says more than any words about their numerical decline. But aside from

| British Railways locomotive stock, 1958-68 | | | | | | | | | | |
	1958	1959	1960	1961	1962	1963	1964	1965	1966	1967	1968
Steam	16,103	14,457	13,276	11,691	8,767	7,050	4,973	2,989	1,689	362	3*
Diesel	1,200	1,799	2,550	3,179	3,683	4,060	4,462	4,811	4,961	4,742	4,325
Electric	72	85	135	158	178	194	198	277	340	341	329

* Vale of Rheidol narrow gauge engines.

drivers and firemen, the attendant workforce associated with the steam railway was huge. Those ten years saw, quite literally, the extinction of a way of life. Management decisions on withdrawal of whole classes of locomotive were handed down from on high. Heretofore, scrapping had been a task undertaken as an orderly part of the railway's process of renewal. Indeed, certain parts were reutilized in new construction to the point that some classes were described as 'rebuilds'. But the laying waste of over 16,000 working locomotives in ten years was a task of a totally different magnitude from anything seen before.

Thus, up to the commencement of those ten years that were to see BR 'out of steam', the task of scrapping life-expired engines was performed, around the country, at the workshops large and small where such tasks had traditionally been undertaken. From Inverurie and St Rollox, Kilmarnock and Cowlairs down through Darlington and Doncaster, Horwich and Crewe; from Gorton and Derby, Wolverhampton Stafford Road and Caerphilly to Swindon and Barry; from Eastleigh, Brighton and Ashford to Stratford and Ryde, all works associated with the main pre-grouping companies performed their sombre role. Sombre, yet dignified; for many of the engines concerned would have lingered often for years, in the twilight world of after-life that was withdrawal, but before dismemberment. Sometimes engines found life as stationary boilers. I well remember the thrill of discovering an ancient North British 0-6-0 thus but recently employed on a visit to St Margarets MPD in Edinburgh in July 1967, 76 years to the month since she emerged new from the Cowlairs works of the North British Railway in 1891.

The BR Modernisation Plan was to change all that. Surgery or even butchery was one thing, but the holocaust of iron inherent in the plan to lay waste 16,000 steam engines needed an operation of a magnitude beyond the capacity, indeed beyond the contemplation, of the BR works. With countless other enthusiasts, I am indebted to Nigel Trevena, founder of Atlantic Publishers, for the research that has gone into his series of books entitled 'Steam for Scrap', from which invaluable works much of the following information is extracted.

Perhaps it was appropriate that Western Region, inheritors of the mantle of the GWR, should lead the rush out of steam and into diesel power.

From Swindon, before first light on 25 March 1959, four of Church-ward's '43xx' Moguls — Nos 5312, 5360, 5392 and 5397 — set off as the first 'train' of dead engines bound for a private scrapyard. Their destination was Woodham Brothers in Barry. Thus began a trickle that soon became a flood, as Britain's major scrapyards identified a source of business to keep them busy for the next decade.

That Dai Woodham's yard was the recipient of the first of these engines was both prophetic, in the light of the unique role played by that yard, and a tribute to the perception of the man himself. Proximity to the steel furnaces of South Wales made the scrapyards there a predictable destination. Buttigieg's and Cashmore's of Newport, Hayes of Bridgend, Bird's of Risca, Ward's of Briton Ferry, Cohen's of Morriston — names formerly unknown to the railway fraternity were soon to become household words, as the railway press recorded monthly purchases. The holocaust of Britain's steam fleet was under way.

There were few more melancholy sights than that of withdrawn locomotives being towed, dead, to their place of dismemberment. Often the motive power was provided by an engine itself performing its last revenue-earning duty for BR, like someone driving themselves to their own funeral.

In Sonning Cutting on 2 November 1963, 'Hall' Class 4-6-0 No 4950 Patshull Hall pulled an unidentified sister, unkempt, rusty, vandalized but dignified, down the slow line, late on a sunny autumn afternoon. Silent, private grief.

Opposite *Epitaph to the world's most famous scrapyard. It is hard to prove, but it is fair to claim, that more films have been used, more photographs taken, at Barry than at any other scrapyard on earth. To Dai Woodham, seen here between '8F' 2-8-0 No 48173 and BR Standard '4' 2-6-0 No 76084 on 4 July 1980, perhaps falls the title of Britain's last 'Man of Steam'. My association with him has been both fulfilling and enduring.*

Both these engines survive to live another day. Solitude amongst the Barry engines, silent ranks of stoical steam locomotives, abused, cut and vandalized, was mine to endure.

Competition between the yards was intense. Sale was by competitive tender, with the purchasing yard having also to pay for the cost of the 'dead engine movement' from the last BR resting place to the destination. South Wales, of course, was not the only area where major scrapyards were sited, and engines travelled to their final resting places all over Britain. Long journeys would add to the price, so many, but by no means all, engines were scrapped in the areas from which they were withdrawn. However, particularly as August 1968 — the end of steam — approached, those scrapyards with a large workforce would often outbid a smaller, nearer yard in order to keep men gainfully employed.

It is no part of this chapter to seek to write a potted history of the 'scrapping' of those 16,000 engines. The role of the private scrapyards can, however, be measured by recalling that they acquired 975 of the 999 Standard locomotives built — and scrapped — by BR, whilst only 24 were scrapped in the five BR works of Crewe, Darlington, Eastleigh, Swindon and Stratford.

For the general public, this act of carnage was both invisible and unknown: if they knew, few probably cared. For railway enthusiasts, the appearance of those lists of 'withdrawals' in the monthly columns

of the railway press was a time of deep gloom. Yet, but one month after the end of steam, there occurred an event — again at Woodham's yard in Barry — that was the precursor of steam's Dunkirk: LMS '4F' 0-6-0 No 43924 left *en route* for the Keighley & Worth Valley Railway.

Whilst to enthusiasts the steam holocaust was a tragedy, to BR it was business. In 1963 they raised about £20 million through sales for scrap of locomotives, rolling-stock and track itself, about 12 per cent of their passenger traffic revenue for that year. Yet it was not only locomotives themselves that were scrapped: items of metal known today as 'railwayana', which are sold for high prices at auctions, were sold for a song, given away, or purloined. It was common to see locomotives withdrawn, stored, or awaiting scrap, intact with numberplates and even nameplates until the final year of steam. But by then, the cutter's torch was raised, not deliberately to remove an item but, in determination, to destroy.

On Thursday 9 November 1989, it was my privilege to 'celebrate' the departure of the last steam engine from Dai Woodham's yard. Barry had indeed witnessed an escape of Dunkirk-like proportions. It was a saga that, in the annals of railway history, will surely be unique.

Bulleid's 'Q1' 0-6-0s were never pretty engines, in steam, any time, any where. They were, nevertheless, 40 of the most distinctive locomotives ever to run on Britain's railways. On 3 October 1964, No 33007 has reached the end of the line, seen here at Feltham with the author in attendance. She was withdrawn in January 1964 and scrapped at Cashmore's, Newport, that December.

Other dated features — not counting my narrow tie — include the signal box, the telegraph pole and the wooden-bodied goods truck. No 33007 has gone: her numberplate survives, thanks to the help of Feltham's erstwhile shedmaster, my good friend, Ted Richardson, the photographer.

8
EPILOGUE ... OR EPITAPH?

'Out of Steam' may be a useful *double entendre* to encapsulate both the end of the steam era, and an implication of exhaustion. One argument far from exhausted, however, is the debate about the future *ownership* of Britain's railways. If vehemence were equated with knowledge, or enthusiasm with dispassion, then the debate would be conducted intelligently. Unfortunately, as so often happens, political prejudice breeds more heat than light. In all the dogmatic clamour of the argument, two groups of people seem to be omitted from participation, namely those who depend on the railway, and those who work on the railway.

When asked for my views on the 'privatization' of British Rail, I invite my questioner to tell me the *purpose* of such an act. This seems, more often than not, to create confusion. It is as though the proposers feel that one should automatically comprehend the purpose. There are indeed some good reasons for transferring industries from the public to the private sector; but there are bad reasons, too. In endeavouring to conduct, in this final chapter, a sensible, balanced discussion, let me try to set out the arguments adduced for and against and test their validity. I hasten to add that these are not my assumptions, but rather are they the assumptions of those on either wing of the argument. Here goes:

For
1. Public ownership is bad in principle and should be terminated regardless of any other consideration.
2. The taxpayer would be saved huge sums of money currently supplied to BR.
3. Private sector management, with its market discipline, would provide better service to the customer.
4. Removal of BR from Treasury investment and spending controls would enable long-term planning to be undertaken and carried through without the risk of political interference and cancellation.
5. There is scope for more new lines to be built which BR is unwilling to build, due to lack of initiative or lack of funds or inability to meet Government investment criteria.

6. Competition will be stimulated, to the benefit of the customer.
7. Industrial relations are handled better outside the public sector.

Against
1. Public ownership of vital national industrial undertakings is essential, regardless of any other consideration.
2. Passenger railways worldwide are a public service. Many sectors can never be 'profitable'; no nation has discovered a formula to make them so; the private sector cannot provide these services without public sector grant.
3. As shown in this book, obligations laid on the railways, ranging from wartime emergency to safety, set them apart from other forms of land transport. (Why do not roads have signals, separating traffic by gaps?)
4. The waste of resources inherent in a multiplicity of railway companies led to the 'Grouping' in 1923, and eventually to nationalization, following wartime bankruptcy. Only now is a 'national' system emerging, and fragmentation would be bad. On a small island like Britain, there is no room for more than one railway to link the main centres efficiently.
5. 'Solutions' such as a Track Authority to own the track would lead a) to the creation of a body to determine who has what rights, where to run which trains, and when; and b) to endless duplication of

In February 1963, in the early weeks of my railway photography, a visit to Willesden Junction High Level station — then still extant — and to Willesden MPD brought poor reward in terms of light, but much of interest. Here, an unidentified '9F' 2-10-0 runs tender-first, light engine, on the bridge across the West Coast Main Line and adjacent tracks.

On the extreme left is the awning and platform of the Low Level station; the locomotive is about to pass beneath an ancient LNWR signal gantry; more 'modern' semaphores guard the tracks nearest the camera; and the signal-box on the extreme right reminds us that much of the old pre-Grouping railway was all around.

There exists no finer or more noble epitaph to the steam era than the Great Western 'Castle' Class 4-6-0s. Introduced in 1923, these magnificent machines were the envy of their jealous rivals and the pride of everyone who worked for or used the GWR. In fact, construction of the class continued into the British Railways era, the last emerging in 1950. My amateurish attempts at panning would disqualify this picture on normal considerations; but even this handicap, plus the disfigurement of the double chimney, merits a place in this chapter for No 7023 Penrice Castle at speed near Twyford with the 11.10 Saturday Worcester-Paddington express on 29 June 1963.

vehicles between competing companies.

6. True 'competition' can only exist on separate railway systems serving the same end-to-end destinations on different tracks.

7. The Department of Transport has not had its doors knocked down by investors wanting to build new railways. All that would happen would be 'asset stripping', resulting in closure of the unprofitable routes or their retention by means of public subsidy which negates the financial arguments in favour of privatization.

As I write down these 'For' and 'Against' arguments — which, let me repeat, are not to be taken as my views — my consciousness of the importance of history as a guide, and of experience elsewhere, moulds my view. Such 'research', or at least knowledge based on an interest in railway history, is neither available to, sought, nor required by most of those, mainly politicians, who hold strong views on the subject. Such thoughts were much in my mind as, on Wednesday 5 October 1988, I set off by rail from London to Shrewsbury on the Great Western Railway.

Formerly part of the trunk route from Paddington to Birkenhead via Banbury, Birmingham, Wolverhampton Low Level, Shrewsbury, Wrexham and Chester, few if any, other than a fanatic like me, would today leave Paddington to reach Shrewsbury; yet the journey and its memories encapsulate the changes made to our national railway network since the Beeching era. The journey — or journeys, comprising London to Newport and then to Shrewsbury — included more than just memories. The two-car 'Sprinter' units rostered for the Crewe-Cardiff trains vividly illustrate the outcome of a policy forced on the railways by Government, which puts economy as a priority, rather than service. That the Cardiff-Crewe train was running 20 minutes late was due to the failure of the rostered 'Sprinter' unit caused, so I was told, by overworked units being run into the ground, too few units for the traffic requirement being a direct result of the reduction in the Public Service Obligation (PSO) grant for the cross-country services. Last, but by no means least, was the conversation enjoyed with the 'conductor-guard', to use the current job-description, and his travelling companion, both epitomizing the commitment to 'the railway' which is still the hallmark of most railwaymen.

That conversation would be reasonably familiar to those who care about our railway system. Even with modernization, enormously improved productivity, and tamed militant trade unionism — I do not want to cause offence, but this is a reasonable description of changes in the railway industry — the railway still depends heavily on its people for its success. Whilst the intense personal loyalty felt by, shall we say (naturally), the men of the GWR to *their* company may not have

Swindon station, in 1971, had lost its style, had yet to be rebuilt, and was merely grim. Western Region's 'Western' Class diesel locomotives were no match for the style of the 'Kings' and 'Castles' of the GWR, but compared to other regions' motive power at least maintained that Railway's touch of distinctiveness. Note the loudspeaker, top left, and the arrows and triangles atop the station building on the right.

The Oxted area, once a twilight zone, was provided with 19 three-car diesel multiple units built in 1962. They gradually replaced the Maunsell 'Moguls' and BR Standards on the passenger services. On 13 April 1963, for some unknown reason, I photographed unit No 1317 approaching the staggered platform at Edenbridge on a Redhill train. The Ashford-Tonbridge-Redhill line was spared by Beeching, for future Channel Tunnel usage.

As yet, BR cannot meet the Government's investment criteria enabling them fully to modernize the line and incorporate it into the Channel Tunnel rail network, making Beeching seem generous. Note the semaphore signal and telegraph pole; trademarks of yesteryear.

been transferred *sine qua non* to the Western Region of British Rail, there remains instilled in many railwaymen the feeling of identity with their industry which is a matter of satisfaction. Many younger railwaymen enjoy the connection with their forebears expressed subconsciously through the continuity of metal wheels on metal tracks. Indeed, repainted and renewed 'company' insignia, on BR property, are readily apparent to the observant — on the platform of Cardiff Station (GWR!), seats have been picked out in new paint.

Whilst nothing can replace the *esprit de corps* of the steam era, whilst never can be repeated the relationship 'twixt terminus-arriving passengers with driver and fireman leaning out of their cab at the buffers, there still exists the basis of a sound relationship. The crew want to bring in their train on time. This attitude may legitimately be described as public service. How many of the 'Privatization Brigade' think of such things?

Inevitably in this chapter, there is the risk of my repeating thoughts and ideas expressed earlier in the book. The seven 'for' and 'against' propositions enumerated above were merely my attempt to set down on paper the parameters within which to discuss the thesis of privatization. As a Member of Parliament closely identified with 'the railway', I am in a privileged position. When I first began this chapter, at the end of 1988, the arguments for and against were just beginning. The

main 'players' were and will be the Secretary of State for Transport, and the Chairman of British Rail: at the time of writing, Cecil Parkinson and Sir Robert Reid respectively. The former has held the job since the cabinet reshuffle of 1989, whilst Sir Robert retired in March 1990, to be replaced by his namesake Bob Reid of Shell. Thus between the preparation of the manuscript and the publication of *Out of Steam*, much has changed. Fortunately, however, we are still a good away from any specific legislative action, or even legislative proposal. Fortunately, also, the characters of the two men who were *in situ* at the commencement of the evaluation process should ensure that the process gets under way without the early establishment of entrenched positions from which any deviation is dubbed as 'retreat'. On the political front, the failure of the Government's attempt to sell off the nuclear sector of the electricity industry, combined with growing public hostility to dogmatic politics, may save BR from becoming a political football. But some of my Parliamentary colleagues still hanker after their perceived Valhalla.

At the end of this chapter's opening paragraph, reference was made to two vital groups of people, namely those who work on, and those who depend upon, the railway. Having made reference to the former, let us look at the matter from the perspective of the latter, namely the railway's customers. As a segregated entity, they do not exist; the millions of people involved represent the total cross-section of the British

The changing scene at King's Cross. It can only have been the need to finish a reel of film that roused me to take this shot, of another characterless DMU emerging from Gasworks Tunnel. A Brush Type 2 — I think — stands on the left.

people, and a substantial and increasing number of foreign tourists, too. Indeed, the image of BR from the viewpoint of the latter is substantially different from the vantage point of the commuter on the Dartford loop-line, especially if said overseas tourist hails from that land of the private railway, the United States of America. The truth surely is that the overwhelming majority of the railway's customers care not who *owns* the system. Their interest is solely concentrated on performance and on value for money. Whilst the tourist enjoying first class travel to York may view the product differently from the rush-hour commuter, they are both exercising *choice*. It is pointless and unrealistic to expect the London rush-hour commuter to be able to enjoy the same style and standard as the long-distance off peak 'voluntary' traveller. The fact is, the commuter does have a choice: he does not have to work in London; he does not have to live 20, 30, 40 miles from his place of work; he could go all or part of the way by car, or motorcycle, or cycle, or bus. Commuting is an option exercised as the least difficult, or *per se* as the most acceptable, method of undertaking a selected journey to a chosen destination to fulfil one's personal role in the firmament. British Rail did not invent the 'rush-hour'.

If you accept my proposition, therefore, that BR's customers are concerned with how the railway serves them, rather than who owns the system, we have turned our minds to Proposition Number 1 on my list of 'for' and 'against' criteria.

Having listed these seven criteria, perhaps it is necessary to elaborate on some of the others, although they are not designed to, nor indeed do they, balance each other. This process of examination continues in various forums at Westminster and its environs. The task of BR management during this debate is not easy. On the one hand they must undertake their main function of running the railway, without embroiling themselves in politics. On the other, they must provide information, not just to Civil Servants in the Department of Transport, and to Ministers therein, but also to backbench Members of Parliament. Amongst the latter, many but not all seem entrenched in their views in accordance with their political affiliations. They — we — fall into three categories, two of them being those who believe, simplistically, that Item 1 'for' or Item 1 'against' in my list is the beginning and end of the argument.

I do not believe that either Item 1 'for' or Item 1 'against' is acceptable or correct. Indeed, either 'analysis' is simplistic, ignorant, intellectually unsustainable and frankly insulting to the intelligence of the electorate — and by 'electorate' I refer *pari passu* to BR's customer. That is not to say that the debate is futile; so to believe would be to believe that BR is perfect, unimprovable, beyond criticism. Would that this were the case; it is not. However, it has to be said that 'the great debate' is, for the most part, being conducted by or within groups whose motto might best be delineated in the phrase: 'Don't confuse me with the facts. I have already made up my mind'. One is as likely to find the framework for intellectual honesty and open-mindedness in the Adam Smith Institute (ASI) or the Centre for Policy Studies (CPS), as in the Executive of the NUR or ASLEF. Unfortunately — or perhaps not! — the former two bodies do not contain people on whom the running of the railways is dependent. Peter Semmens, in checking the proofs of this book, stated: 'I was at a conference in May at which someone spoke as the Transport Consultant for the ASI. His grasp of facts was abysmal.'

As substantiation of this serious charge, let me quote from a document put out by one of my more cerebral colleagues, in his report of a conference held to 'discuss' the subject of railway privatization, in the autumn of 1988. Naturally, being suspected of having an open mind, I was not invited to participate! The 'conference' was not conducting a 'debate'; it was a mass soliloquy. The only issue was *how* to privatize, not *whether* so to do. The report of that CPS soliloquy was entitled 'Signals from a Railway Conference'. It contains comments disguised as 'facts' which highlight their authors' ignorance. British Rail is accused of 'failing' to use its monopoly position to drive routes underground across London. Anyone familiar with the financial circumstances surrounding the building of such lines would understand why the Treasury has in fact even in 1989 specifically rejected the proposal to do precisely as is recommended, namely to build an underground line from Paddington to Liverpool Street. This is not a failure of BR, it is a failure of the Government to recognise transport priorities.

Reference is made to BR being under strong competition from road transport, yet no attempt is made to ask whether it is fair competition. BR is criticized for raising fares to the level the market can bear (somewhat surprising when such criticism emanates from Thatcherite sources!). But it is then suggested that one of the protections to be built into privatization should be safeguards to cope with the fact that 'the captive commuter in particular will demand a measure of stability under a privatized regime.'

There are double standards of substantial proportions here; on the one hand, a nationalized industry is criticized for charging market prices, whilst on the other, privatization is advocated which will necessitate inbuilt price-fixing.

The 'conference' was told that city funds would be made available for investment 'providing first that a system of grants was formalized so that shareholders would know what support was going to be available from the Government'. Let us hope that the 'support' that might be forthcoming will be more appealing to the city than that offered by the Government in its discarded plan to privatize the nuclear sector of the electricity supply industry.

The confusion in the minds of the contributors and authors of this document is nowhere better illustrated than their comments on the reasons why, on the one hand, uneconomic rail services were discontinued and, on the other, investment has not been forthcoming to build new railways like the TGV in France. The authors cover this whole subject in one sentence: 'The difficulties of closing down old routes and services has led to a reluctance to set up new ones.' What on earth is the relationship between, say, the closure of the Higham Ferrers branch in 1959 and the environmental difficulties of financing the Channel Tunnel rail link today?

Our great free marketeers included in their discussion of the subsidy question the following sentence: 'A pledge to keep prices rising at no more than the general rate of inflation would bring about a very much better state of affairs than we see now.' Approximately, therefore, the *nationalized* industry can continue to set its prices according to what the market can bear, but a *privatized* industry would be subject to the full panoply of the prices section of an as yet undetermined prices and incomes policy.

I won't embarrass my colleague who wrote the document — now a junior member of the Government — by quoting his name, but the whole event was put into context by the opening sentence of the then Secretary of State for Transport, Paul Channon, who said: 'I want to emphasize at the start that Her Majesty's Government has not decided to privatize British Rail. There is no chance of doing so in the life-time of this Parliament'.

It is obvious that Mr Channon had looked into the problems rather more carefully and analytically than the Centre for Policy Studies. No wonder some think that the CPS is to the Conservative party what the Militant Tendency is to the Labour Party. Perhaps that is why I deleted the word 'Railway' and replaced it with 'Political' when a copy of 'Signals from a Railway Conference' reached me. It is no more open-minded than papers from 'Transport 2000' or the rail unions.

Thus, at this early stage of the Parliamentary debate, let me conclude with an attempt to encompass the 'for' and 'against' points listed above. I have dealt with the question of *ownership*, and, briefly, with the question of *politics*. The other main areas of debate can, perhaps, be covered by the headings of *finance*, *competition*, *national interest* and *investment*. Let us examine them briefly, in that order, taking finance first.

As the demand for new railway lines asserts itself, to cope with modern phenomena ranging from the Channel Tunnel, road congestion, population changes and new towns, to name but four, it is worth casting our minds back to the early railway years. The Parliamentary process has altered little, but the invention of the internal combustion engine has, in reality, utterly transformed the environment, both literally and that within which the argument is taking place. That railway transport has survived at all, in the age of the car, the coach, the aeroplane, the juggernaut, is a miracle. It might have been supposed that the internal combustion engine and the aircraft would do to the railways in Britain what the railways themselves did to the canals. But it is not so. Indeed, the car, coach and lorry that, not long ago, looked like the grave-diggers for rail travel, are now, due to their very proliferation and creation of congestion and pollution, likely to be its saviour.

The problems faced by railway promoters today are a magnification of those faced by their forebears 150 years ago. Lessons painfully learned by, for example, the Great Western and Cheltenham Union Railway in the face of opposition from Squire Robert Gordon of Kemble, who demanded and obtained a tunnel where the Company's line proposed to pass by his Kemble House, and who forced the Company to locate its original Kemble Station outwith the boundary of his estate, are not dissimilar from the problems being encountered, at the time of writing, by British Rail as they seek an acceptable new line across Kent for Channel Tunnel trains. The same issues affect the plans to redevelop and rebuild King's Cross. Costs are increased very substantially by such environmental and self-interested considerations. The same problems will be faced by any railway promoters today. Yet, in the era of the private car in an overcrowded island, does it *really* make sense for a modern Government and Parliament to apply the criteria of the 1840s to the 1990s? In those early years of Victoria's reign, financial, not environmental, criteria were the main problem for the railway promoters. They were pushing at the frontiers of technology for material gain, rather than seeking to provide an answer to the congestion and pollution created by cars, coaches and lorries.

If private capital is mobilized to build new railway lines to and through — or under — the towns, cities and countryside of Britain today, where shall we draw the boundary 'twixt private interest and public benefit? Can or should Government merely shrug its shoulders and stand aside from the process? In considering the financial implications of railway privatization, the public interest cannot be ignored: if it is, we shall neither get the railways we need, nor shall we be able to modernize and improve the existing system. I ask again — why do we fund roads out of taxation, yet expect railways to be 'profitable'?

The word 'competition' springs readily to the lips of the Privatization Brigade as their primary totem. (These words are being written on the evening on which a bus company called 'Charlie's Cars', based in Dorset, and a product of deregulation, ran its final services: it is being wound up for financial reasons.) The word 'competition' implies a 'winner' and a 'loser': it does not, in itself, encompass any element of 'fairness' in reaching conclusions. A conversation with the recently appointed Minister for Public Transport, Michael Portillo, however, was encouraging. He accepts that his Department's traditional criteria for comparing the 'costs' of road as opposed to rail investment are not 'fair'. So far, so good. This point is made as part of the case against those claiming the need for greater competition as a reason for privatizing the railway. So, I repeat — 'Why privatize?' If competition between rail and its 'competitors' is not based on fair criteria, let us change the criteria before we can measure the validity of claims about competitive travel.

If 'external' competitors to the railways cannot be, or are not, fairly measured what are the prospects for 'internal' competition? This is where

Opposite *Common survivors from the LNER classes as steam's nadir approached were the Thompson 'B1' 4-6-0s. Introduced in 1942, they became the LNER's most numerous class. Were it not for their contemporaneity with Stanier's 'Black Five', and the sullenness of reputation enjoyed by their designer, more would perhaps have been written about the 'B1'. Unlike the tapered variety of the Stanier engine, Thompson's machine had a parallel boiler. In all, 409 of the class were built.*

When I took this photograph of 'B1' No 61394 at King's Cross Top Shed in March 1963, my photography had just begun, and Top Shed's reputation for cleanliness was still evident, even though the shed would soon close. Sporting its 34A shedplate, No 61394, built late on in January 1952, was, however, about to be transferred from King's Cross to 41D Canklow in a few days' time. Although only 11 years old, would she ever be so clean again?

the fanatics enter the scene, the loudness of their claims usually matched by the shallowness of their knowledge or the paucity of their thought about the subject. One recently-elected Conservative MP was firm in his belief that BR needed the 'stimulus' of 'competition' to 'transform' its performance. At a private dinner as the guest of BR's chairman, Bob Reid, in late November 1988, he asserted his beliefs with vigour. 'If British Airways in private hands can transform itself from loss to profit, so can BR,' he trumpeted. Untrammelled by knowledge of 150 years' legislation and obligation placed by Parliament on the railways; oblivious to the minor differences inherent in transport modes based on flying through the air or running on fixed tracks; and certainly not having thought about the effect on railway finances and prospects wrought, since their invention, by the internal combustion engine, let alone the aeroplane, he pressed his case. Quietly, kindly, Bob Reid confronted him with reality. Gently he prodded the balloon of confidence with the pinprick of reality. Slowly, the bombast subsided. By the end of dinner, our hero was reduced to proposing the introduction of competitive catering services on the trains!

Is there, on the ground of competition, a case to be made for 'privatization'? Did the pre-or-post-grouping era offer the trail traveller a better service than is available today? If so, can we re-create those days in the current climate?

Students of railway history — a group of people which, sadly, lacks many members in the House of Commons, if not in the House of Lords — will recall the fabled 'Railway Races', the heroic efforts of the East Coast and West Coast Companies competing on the London-Edinburgh run. On 1 June 1888, the West Coast Companies began to run their principal day trains between the two capitals in nine instead of ten hours. The rival route operated by the East Coast Companies, which since 1876 had had a nine-hour service, then reduced their booked time to 8½ hours. Towards the end of July, the West Coast announced that their timings would be reduced to 8½ hours as from 1 August, whereupon, on said date, the East Coast reduced their timing to eight hours. On 6 August, the West Coast companies matched *this* time, but in order so to do reduced their train to a featherweight four carriages, weighing but 80 tons.

This was not the end of the affair. On 13 August 1888, the East Coast reduced their timing to 7¾ hours, whilst on that very day the West Coast ran a train from Euston to Edinburgh in 7 hours 38 minutes. The following day, the East Coast run was completed in 7 hours 32 minutes. This great contest was fought in a blaze of public interest; just imagine what the television era would have made of it all! Then, with the formal opening of the Forth Bridge on 4 March 1890 by the Prince of Wales, the battleground moved northwards. Aberdeen was the new target. Yet again, the protagonists — London & North Western and Caledonian Railways on the West Coast, and Great Northern, North Eastern and North British Railways on the East Coast — slugged

Nottingham Midland station has survived, whilst Victoria has, to belated lamentations, disappeared as a transport artery, sunk under a sea of sickly concrete. On 16 July 1964, LMS Fairburn 2-6-4T No 42221 pulls into Midland station with empty stock beneath the bridge that carried GCR tracks. What a filthy state the engine is in.

I did not visit this station again until the day of the Great Wind, 25 January 1990. Our return from Lincoln to King's Cross became a cross-country nightmare via Nottingham Midland and, eventually, St Pancras.

it out nightly from Euston and King's Cross respectively to Aberdeen; or, to be strictly accurate, to the point at Kinnaber Junction, 38 miles south of Aberdeen, where the two lines from the south converged.

Such was the world in which genuine competition existed on Britain's railways. In order to replace an era in which such competition excited the interest and attention of the customer, it would be necessary to do one or two things:

a) un-invent the aeroplane

b) dig up all motorways, bypasses, etc

c) un-invent the internal combustion engine

d) re-open the stretches of track, such as the Strathmore line, closed in order to avoid wasteful duplication

e) find investors willing to put their funds into a railway system without the benefit of a), b) and c) above.

Doubtless there are more items one could identify if one attempted to create, or to re-create, 'internal' rail competition. The absolutely fundamental criterion for such competition, as mentioned elsewhere in this book is the ability to offer competing services between two end-point cities via different routes: thus Euston to Edinburgh Princes Street via Crewe versus King's Cross to Edinburgh Waverley via Grantham; Euston to Birmingham New Street via Rugby (LNWR) versus Paddington to Birmingham Snow Hill via Banbury (GWR); Waterloo to Exeter Queen St via Salisbury (LSWR) versus Paddington to Exeter St Davids via Taunton (GWR); St Pancras to Nottingham Midland via Luton (Midland) versus Marylebone to Nottingham Victoria via Aylesbury (GCR).

Internal rail competition — genuine, not manufactured — cannot be created on the same tracks. A railway line is not like Brands Hatch, or even the M1; for a start it is a great deal safer, and that safety is provided at the cost of the railway company, not the taxpayer. However, it is not at all difficult to improve the *competitiveness* of rail towards its *external* competitors. All that is needed is money. The French TGV has decimated the competition from the airlines on the Paris-Lyon route. SNCF, however, is state-owned, not a point to be emphasized too loudly to the Privatization Brigade.

One way that competition in some form might be created is what in shorthand one might call the 'Pullman Route'. Pullman cars were first introduced into Britain by the Midland Railway in 1874. Although the Midland discontinued their inclusion in its trains in 1888, other railway companies took up the use of the distinctively liveried carri-

Yeovil Junction remains thus, and is invaluable. This early morning departure for Waterloo behind a Class '50' diesel locomotive repays careful study.

The line to Yeovil Pen Mill and Castle Cary is that curving away at bottom right; it is officially a freight-only line at this point. The Class '50' is not working 'wrong line'; this is a reversible section of double line, eastwards to Sherborne and Templecombe, and this 'up' train has departed from what, at initial glance, would appear logically to be the 'down' platform at Yeovil Junction station.

In the left background remains a small goods yard. To the left of the locomotive, the proposed new Clifton Maybank curve will provide direct access from the Weymouth line, into Yeovil Junction.

ages of the Pullman Car Company. In 1881, the London, Brighton & South Coast Railway introduced an all-Pullman train between London and Brighton. Forerunner of the luxurious 'Southern Belle', LB & SCR Pullman services survived into Southern Railway days and on into BR Southern Region; well do I remember the feeling of style and superiority enjoyed by paying 1/6d (7½p) extra and travelling Pullman from Brighton to Victoria. But Pullmans were not a *competitor* to the railways; they were nothing more than a marketing attraction, like First Class on an airline. Nevertheless, they were indeed an attraction, and BR would do well to consider introducing the name on many more trains than they do at present, and indeed allowing a private sector operator to offer the service, under the Pullman name, or indeed any other. The insertion of a Pullman coach on 'ordinary' service trains, as practised by the SR on their south coast services from Victoria and London Bridge with their 6-PUL units, is an option that should be assessed again.

Having touched on competition, let us now turn to an examination of national interest. This aspect of the question has already been dealt with quite extensively in an earlier chapter ('Who Needs a Railway?'). Perhaps the question can best be addressed by reference to a conversation enjoyed in the preparation for this book, with two men actively involved in running (down) the railway in the aftermath of Beeching, Sid Keeling, to whom reference has already been made, and Bert Harrison.

Sid Keeling joined the LMS in 1937, and observed the Beeching years from his position as Divisional Operating Superintendent at Euston on the London Midland Region. It was at his suggestion that Bert Harrison joined us. Railwaymen are by nature loyal to their fellows and to their industry, and are rarely men of hyperbole or exaggeration. Thus, the opportunity of talking to Bert Harrison was of great value: in 1966, following a career that commenced on the LNER in 1942, he completed a course at Manchester Business School prior to taking up a crucial role at BR Board Headquarters. His position was entitled 'Assistant Reshaping Officer'.

The overall impression of talking to him was that the railwaymen of the Beeching era — or at least those charged with the task of implementing the Beeching closures — became numbed to their task. In response to my question as to whether he and his colleague were 'selecting the lines to be closed, or administering their closure', he stated, 'Administering: the blue book listed the ones to be closed.'

'The first step we had to take was to publish a notice in *The Times* and *The Daily Telegraph*. One month later, the Region had to put up a notice saying that the line was going to be closed and anyone who wished to object had to contact the Transport Users Consultative Committee. The TUCC then had to decide whether or not to hold a hearing. If there were a lot of objections, they held a hearing. Its role was to allow the public to vent its wrath, and then the closure could pro-

ceed. Next the TUCC drew up a report which went to the Minister of Transport and to the Board. I then became involved, dealing with the Ministry of Transport and considering with them and the Regions alternative services, eg bus services, how many buses, etc.'

He was not trying in any way to be cynical: he would rightly object if I should so describe his prosaic explanation of his allotted task. In retrospect, Beeching's 'solution' to the problem, cutting 5,000 route miles, closing more than 2,000 stations and reducing passenger routes, was, as Lord Marsh said, 'based on the misconception that the financial problems of the railways could be eradicated by identifying the loss-making services and closing them'. It was a short-sighted 'solution' to a 'problem' of the chicken-and-egg variety. Not much has changed in the minds of certain people, especially those who rarely use trains and do not know what it means to have to rely on them. In the House of Commons, on Tuesday 31 January 1989, I asked the Prime Minister if she would agree that when the Department of Transport

Literally steam's last gasp. At Croes Newydd on 20 March 1966, '57xx' Class pannier tank No 3709 has just performed her last duty prior to the shed's closure. With Western Region having 'managed' to eliminate steam officially by the end of 1965, former GWR motive power hung on at a handful of erstwhile Great Western sheds transferred to London Midland Region territory under BR's occasional divisional reorganizations. Croes Newydd was one such depot.

SPECIAL NOTICE

Parcels facilities are withdrawn from this station

The nearest available station with parcel facilities is

Bolton

Should collection of forwarded parcels be required please telephone

Bolton 382814

≷ British Rail

Epilogue . . . or epitaph?

Opposite *'The loneliness of the long-distance runner.' Stanier '8F' 2-8-0 No 48754 stands in solitary splendour in the broad acres of Whitemoor Yard, March, on 4 February 1964. Once the largest marshalling yard in Britain, its development created the need for a second engine shed. Officially, March Shed (31B) closed to steam some weeks earlier, but my camera told differently.*

Whitemoor confirmed March as the strategic hub of East Anglian freight activity, and the town, although less well-known than most of its fellows, has always been a 'railway town'.

is assessing the true cost to the nation of investment in road versus rail, all the costs should be taken into account? Further, would she agree that, for example, the amount of time that the police force spends on administering the law and dealing with endless problems in the courts is a major cost to the taxpayer? Finally, I asked whether she would instruct the Department of Transport that from now on these and other appropriate costs must be taken into account when the various comparative costs are assessed.

The Prime Minister replied: 'Obviously I agree that all relevant costs should be taken into account, but very many more people and goods go by road than go by rail. My Hon Friend may wish that many more would go by rail, and indeed we are trying to improve the rail service so that that is so. But I accept that all relevant costs should be taken into account, although we may not agree on precisely what the relevant costs are.'

Quite so: if you kick a chap when he is on the ground he may find it more difficult to get to his feet. Or, if you prefer another analogy, if you tie chains to a chap's ankles, he finds his movement hindered; for this is the effect of political decisions taken by successive governments, as the railways have sought to overcome the dice loaded against them. The trouble with the Prime Minister's answer to me is that she does not relate the level of traffic to the unfair investment criteria, but seems to blame the railway — for being treated unfairly. This is to turn facts upside down.

Bert Harrison and Sid Keeling were railwaymen acting at the behest of politicians. Sid gave a typical example of a closure that typifies the penny-pinching attitude, namely the closure of a stretch of track that can prove invaluable in case of a blockage or maintenance work on a busy section.

'I was directly involved with the closure of the Blisworth-Northampton line. The General Manager had his saloon out, looking at the line. We were having lunch and he said to me, 'Now then Keeling, what about this piece of line?' I spent the rest of lunch trying to think of a justification for the line. Everyone else had finished eating and I was trying to catch up! As an operator, you looked for loops in case the main line was ever blocked.'

In spite of the logical protests of the professional railwayman, the line concerned was closed, the infrastructure destroyed and its reinstatement prevented for ever. How on earth is this sensible or 'fair' to the nation?

Whilst the Pullman option provides an additional attraction to passenger services, but is not a *competitor* to BR, two other *non sequiturs*, cited as providing 'evidence' of the role of competition, are mentioned by the Privatization Brigade. One of these is the 'success' of privately preserved railway lines like the Mid-Hants, the North Yorkshire Moors, or the very well run Severn Valley Railway. The other, on the freight side, is the Foster-Yeoman trains. These 'case histories' can be dealt with in a single paragraph each.

The preserved railways are run almost entirely by volunteer labour, with locomotives often owned and maintained by individuals loosely attached to the railway; they have few if any of the web of public obligations imposed on BR by 150 years of legislative intervention. They exist to provide pleasure and enjoyment to their own army of enthusiasts, who 'play trains' for recreational rather than economic advantage to their members. This is not, of course, to criticize enthusiasts, of whom I am one; merely to point out the futile logic of calling in aid these activities as an argument for privatization of the national railway system.

The Foster-Yeoman trains are an example of what BR already recognizes as an opportunity, namely encouraging private sector operators to provide their own wagons and locomotives for BR staff to run on the national network. Private wagons on the railways go back to the early days of the Stockton & Darlington Railway and in the Second

World War, half a million private owner wagons (mainly coal wagons) were requisitioned 'for the emergency'. This is a sensible system that needs to be encouraged: it is not 'privatizing' the railway. Those who suggest that it is, either do not understand the contractual relationship between Foster-Yeoman and BR, or they do not have a clear idea of what they mean by 'privatization', or they are deluding themselves by their own low levels of expectation. Rather than *competing* with BR, Foster-Yeoman is *feeding* BR, in a thoroughly practical and worthwhile, albeit relatively minuscule, manner.

There are other equally welcome manifestations of private enterprise partnership with BR. As I write these words, the current weekly edition of *The Western Gazette* includes a photograph of a BR Class '47' standing at the head of a train of bulk storage wagons. Headlined 'Their Own Railhead', the news item is an excellent example of the opportunities for private rail traffic handling within the existing BR system. Let me quote the item:

> The first privately owned and operated railhead facility in Dorset for many years has been opened on a Purbeck industrial estate, and offers transit of goods to and from the area by rail.
>
> It provides a much-needed alternative to the over-stretched road network as a means of transporting materials and goods, says live-wire manager Nigel McBay.
>
> It is run by TMW Storage, a recently-formed company engaged in warehousing and distribution.
>
> The company occupies a five-acre site on the thriving Holton Heath Industrial Park, has secured a long-term contract with a leading European manufacturer, and as a result now has a giant warehouse alongside its own rail siding recently constructed, running off the main Poole-Weymouth railway line.
>
> Mr McBay says that the company has a big contract for the importing of fertiliser which is stored at the giant warehouse after being brought in by rail, and then distributed by road to Dorset and Hampshire farms.
>
> But the railhead and multi-functional terminal accommodation means it can offer shipping facilities by rail to any producer or importer. 'We can take bulk materials or manufactured goods in and out by rail for anyone interested, at rates that will certainly compare very favourably with road alternatives,' said Mr McBay.

Nigel McBay's words, in that final sentence, make the point clear beyond peradventure: BR is not a monopoly operator, it is a competitor in the carriage of goods and people.

The final category to be examined, in searching for the holy grail over privatization, is investment. Having discussed the heading of 'finance', my intention here is briefly to examine the investment criteria pursued at present by Her Majesty's Government, and to compare how these might differ from the prevailing regime in a private sector company. To do this one needs to imagine a situation far removed from the normal circumstances surrounding such considerations. If commercial considerations are to be the only criteria by which investment decisions would be made, then the cost of producing BR's timetables and maps would be very substantially reduced, because almost all cross-country, commuter and regional services would be discontinued. As, however, the Government has stated that this is not going to happen, then discussion of 'normal investment criteria' can be suspended *sine die*. Unless the 'national interest' is firmly inserted into the equation; unless it is properly defined; unless priorities are established within such a definition; and unless Government evinces its willingness to fund those priorities, then talk of 'railway privatization' remains an entirely 'political', rather than a 'transport', proposition.

British Rail has no monopoly. Its business is to carry animate and inanimate loads between terminal points. Perfect transport monopoly conditions only prevail when the total supply of transport is sufficient to meet the demand and a transport operator can charge, for conveyance, a rate or fare to the fullest extent of the value of the service, certain in the knowledge that the traffic will neither cease not be diverted to another carrier. Such a monopoly seldom exists, and cannot do so unless a substitute is entirely absent. Public transport that suffers no competition whatsoever from any other form of public transport is prevented from operating as a monopoly so long as there is no regulation or restriction of private transport. The customer with his own available private transport has at his command a substitute for such public transport as is unacceptable to him.

Twice in 1988, Conservative backbenchers put forward proposals for railway privatization. The first time, the Member for Stroud sought leave to bring in a Bill to remove the London rail termini from BR ownership: yes, seriously! He lost. There was no further attempt in 1989.

On the second occasion, on a day when Government Members were present in large numbers for a three-line whip, a mere 109 out of a total of 375 Conservative Members went into the Aye lobby to support a proposal for full-blown privatization of BR. The then Secretary of State, Paul Channon, and his Department can therefore examine the proposition coolly. Whilst there are those in the Conservative Party who wish to privatize at any price, and those in the Labour Party who are equally dogmatic the other way, most of us await evidence that Valhalla, in the form of a reincarnated LNWR, actually exists.

Let me close this chapter, and indeed this book, with a brief résumé of the state of the Big Four private railway companies after the war and immediately prior to nationalization. (Whether the word 'private' in modern terminology is appropriate to describe great national companies with such widespread public obligations is a debatable point.)

During the Second World War, the railways were under Government control. In the years 1941-44 alone they earned profits of £350 million, of which more than half was taken from them to fund the war effort. Expenditure on maintenance and renewals, which should have reflected the enormously increased use of the system for wartime requirements, was restricted severely by Government, notwithstanding excessive wear and tear. The post-war physical and financial state of the Big Four was inevitable. It had everything to do with the war, and little indeed to do with the management of the companies.

Repeating what I have said heretofore, the deed of nationalization was political. The early years of BR were disastrous. Politics, committees, rivalries, lack of clear policy and intention moulded the results, and then the subsequent image, of BR. The 1955 Modernisation Plan saw large sums of money dissipated on items like inadequate diesels, as has been described.

Then followed Beeching, which could — and has — been fairly described as an over-reaction to the preceding events. Whilst many closures could be justified, others certainly could not. Painful lessons were learned, but, sadly, too late to reap the benefit on many lines, closed down and sold out of the public's hands. However, some 25 years after the 1948 nationalization we began at last to get things right. The railway system is now planned on a 'national' rather than a 'company' basis: the customer is now recognized for what he is. Traffic is on the increase, although one can still regret the deliberate decimation of most freight services, in contradistinction to the policy in France. Nearly 200 new stations have opened since the Beeching closures were completed. Optimism and opportunity are the current themes of BR senior management. In July 1988, as the privatization debate began, the Government stock, with which erstwhile GWR, LMS, LNER and SR shareholders were compensated at the date of nationalization, was finally repaid by the Government. The Big Four shareholders did not, in honesty, do too well out of the state takeover.

We have an increasingly modern railway, operating at last reasonably efficiently, and still trying to provide a service to the nation. That, for me, is the key to the future.

The future, however, must be a European future. British Rail's success will surely depend on its ability to be, and to be seen to be, part of an increasingly effective rail challenge, both to the car and to the plane. Last year's undignified scramble for a new chairman served only to highlight the dismal view of the job by the captains of British industry.

Whilst Ministers boast about the level of investment in BR — not mentioning that in the years 1982-88 BR was investing its own earnings, rather than borrowings or Government grant — the facts are that, in 1988, BR's investment per passenger mile was 2.5p; Belgium's state railway invested 3p; the Netherlands 3.6p; whilst capitalist, successful West Germany put 7p through Deutsche Bundesbahn. As *The Independent* said recently: 'The new BR chairman will also have to cope as best he can with levels of subsidy and investment which would make almost all his counterparts on the Continent blanch'.

ADDENDUM

Whether or not this book has been well received — and that is perhaps academic to those who have read thus far — it is certainly a 'different' book from my previous literary efforts in the railway field. Attempting to combine nostalgia and politics proved quite difficult. One condition accepted by the publisher was my insistence on updating the book at the latest opportunity, which meant about four months prior to publication: hardly an ideal timescale within which to operate should any dramatic events intervene. However, as I write these words in May 1990, the inexorable drift away from dependence on more roads and cars as the only 'solution' to our transport problem becomes more evident almost daily.

At Westminster, my one-man railway lobbying campaign continued apace. In March, a 20-year wait for the opportunity fully and thoroughly to debate any matter of my choice was ended by my good fortune in winning the 'Ballot for Motions'. This is pure luck — literally a lottery whereby Mr Speaker picks three numbers at random, the numbers corresponding to the number each Member has selected in the appropriate book in the preceding hour. The first number drawn ensures that the lucky Member has the House at his mercy, on a pre-ordained Friday a couple of weeks later. What power!

With the controversy surrounding the introduction of the Community Charge — which I have consistently opposed — it was tempting to debate Local Government finance. I resisted the temptation. At the root of my objections to the transport policies pursued by successive British governments has been the methods used by the Department of Transport to assess competing claims for investment from public funds as between road and rail. Thus my debate was entitled 'Rail Investment Criteria and Public Transport Policy'.

The terms of the Motion had to be framed carefully. A Motion considered hostile by the relevant Minister would obviously not be acceptable to the Government. A backbencher can insist on the wording for his Motion, but to invite the House to debate a controversial Motion would cause a whip to be put on by the Government to defeat it. To do this on a Friday is not the best way to win friends for one's cause! Discretion and common sense coincided; after consultation with

Michael Portillo, Public Transport Minister, we agreed a form of words. He would have preferred my Motion to contain no mention of French or West German railway investment policy; nor of the recent report of the Central Transport Consultative Committee (CTCC), a government-appointed body, which echoed my sentiments.

Whilst the record of the French Government in developing the Train de Grande Vitesse (TGV) has been covered in Chapter 5, the policy of the West German Christian Democratic Government has been less closely scrutinized. With the political fraternity between Christian Democrats and British Conservatives, the policy of the Bonn Government, even more than that of the French, is — or should be — of greater embarrassment to those currently responsible for British public transport policy. Not only their investment programme but, more significantly, their extensive subsidy to Deutsche Bundesbahn, emphasize the yawning gap that exists in philosophy and in practice between the two governments. Indeed, it is not just the French and West Germans, but virtually all the Western European governments who pursue a policy towards their railways that leaves us isolated. As to whether they are right and we are wrong, or *vice versa*, is for many people a 'political' judgement. On grounds of public transport they are certainly different.

During the debate, I quoted the words of Herr Rudolf Richter, General Manager in London of Deutsche Bundesbahn, in which he referred to the relationship of DB with the West German Government. He said: 'Our Government has started to understand that a railway infrastructure and a railway system is more than just a business. It is part of the health of the people.'

'Attitude' in this context is a political statement. That the attitude of the French and West German, or indeed the Swiss, Italian and other West European governments, towards *their* state railways is different from that extant between BR and HMG cannot be in doubt, and has been the subject of some discussion in this book. Hopefully, however, times are indeed changing. The very success of the economic policies pursued during the 1980s in Britain, with the resultant proliferation of cars, coaches and lorries on the roads, has been the primary cause of the dawning, in the minds of Ministers of the Crown and Members of Parliament, of a new Railway Age. As yet, however, that dawn is but a glimmer — a glimmer noticed with little enthusiasm. The most obvious manifestation is the slow but perceptible change of policy towards the need for some public funding of the essential high-speed link (HSL) between the Channel Tunnel and central London.

Throughout the period of creation of this book, from conception to the moment at which I write these words, successive Transport Secretaries and, of course, the Prime Minister have persisted with their self-delusion that an environmentally-acceptable and transport-sensible HSL can be financed and funded either by the private sector or by BR meeting Government investment criteria. It cannot. It will not. Eventually, hopefully before publication of this tome, common sense will defeat dogma, and the infamous Clause 42 of the Channel Tunnel Act will have been circumvented. In fact, the formula that will be adopted, I prophesy (as I did two years ago), will be the provision of extra funds for Network South-East, on the basis that their customers will benefit from the HSL, not least through alleviated congestion.

What a farce it all is, for those of us who *believe* in rail. Shall we, before the next General Election, have yet another Secretary of State for Transport? Will he recognize the vital, essential role that *only* the railways can fulfil? Will he set aside prejudice against public sector funding? As 'transport' climbs the ladder of electoral significance, could the answer to such questions determine the outcome of future General Elections?

BIBLIOGRAPHY AND ABBREVIATIONS

Banando, José *Trains Oubliés*
Body, Geoffrey *The Railway Era* (Moorland Pub Co, 1982)
Bonavia, Michael R. *British Rail: The First 25 Years* (1981)
Calvert, Roger *The Future of Britain's Railways* (1965)
Cox, E.S. *Locomotive Panorama* (1965)
Defoe, D. *A Tour Through the Whole Island of Great Britain* (1724)
Denton, Rev W. *England in the Fifteenth Century* (1888)
Eaton, R.J. *The Elements of Transport* (1936)
Fairclough & Wills *BR Standard Steam in Close-up*
Fiennes, Gerard *Fiennes on Rails* (David & Charles, 1986)
Gourvish, T.R. *British Railways 1949-73* (Cambridge University Press, 1987)
Hardy, R.N.M. *Beeching: Champion of the Railways?* (Ian Allan, 1989)
Hawkins & Reeve *LMS Engine Sheds* (Wild Swan, 1981)
Hooper, John *LNER Sheds in Camera* (OPC, 1984)
Joy, Stewart *The Train that Ran Away*
Jusserand, J.J. *English Wayfaring Life in the Middle Ages* (1891)
Macaulay, John *Modern Railway Working* (1912)
Parliamentary Papers
Pearson, A.J. *The Railways and the Nation* (1964).
Pendleton, J. *Our Railways* (1894)
Pratt, E.A. *British Railways and the Great War* (Selwyn & Blount 1921)
Regional History of the Railways of Great Britain (David & Charles)
Teal, Paul *BR Standards & Austerities* (Ian Allan, 1985)
Trevenna, Nigel *Steam for Scrap* (Atlantic, 1985)
Warren, A. *Rescued from Barry* (David & Charles, 1983)
Williamson, J.W. *Railways Today* (1938)

APT	Advanced Passenger Train
ASI	Adam Smith Institute
ASLEF	Associated Society of Locomotive Engineers and Firemen
BR	British Rail
BTC	British Transport Commission
CLC	Cheshire Lines Committee

CME	Chief Mechanical Engineer
CPS	Centre for Policy Studies
DB	Deutsche Bundesbahn
DLR	Docklands Light Railway
dmu	Diesel multiple unit
GCR	Great Central Railway
GNR	Great Northern Railway
GWR	Great Western Railway
HMG	Her Majesty's Government
LBSCR	London, Brighton & South Coast Railway
LMS	London Midland & Scottish (Railway)
LNER	London & North Eastern Railway
LNWR	London & North Western Railway
L & Y	Lancashire and Yorkshire (Railway)
MPD	Motive power depot
MR	Midland Railway
MSWJ	Midland & South Western Junction (Railway)
NAO	National Audit Office
NB	North British (Railway)
NBL	North British Locomotive Company
NUR	National Union of Railwaymen
PLM	Paris-Lyon Mediterannée
PO-Midi	Paris-Orléans Railway
PSO	Public Service Obligation
RCTS	Railway Correspondence & Travel Society
S & D	Somerset & Dorset (Joint Railway)
SECR	South Eastern & Chatham Railway
SNCF	Société National des Chemins de Fer
SR	Southern Region
TUCC	Transport Users' Consultative Committee
TGV	Train de Grande Vitesse
TGV/A	Train de Grande Vitesse Atlantique
TGV/N	Train de Grande Vitesse Nord
TGV/PSE	Train de Grande Vitesse Paris Sud-Est
WD	War Department

INDEX

Page numbers in *italics* refer to illustrations. Locomotives featured therein are included in the index, but only exceptionally when mentioned in the text. Places and people germane to the narrative are also included. However, to avoid excessive repetition, neither BR, nor GWR, LMS, LNER or SR, is included.